USING
DATA

To Focus
Instructional
Improvement

USING DATA

To Focus Instructional Improvement

Cheryl James-Ward
Douglas Fisher
Nancy Frey
Diane Lapp

Alexandria, Virginia USA

1703 N. Beauregard St. • Alexandria, VA 22311-1714 USA
Phone: 800-933-2723 or 703-578-9600 • Fax: 703-575-5400
Website: www.ascd.org • E-mail: member@ascd.org
Author guidelines: www.ascd.org/write

Gene R. Carter, *Executive Director;* Mary Catherine (MC) Desrosiers, *Chief Program Development Officer;* Richard Papale, *Publisher;* Genny Ostertag, *Acquisitions Editor;* Julie Houtz, *Director, Book Editing & Production;* Darcie Russell, *Editor;* Sima Nasr, *Senior Graphic Designer;* Mike Kalyan, *Production Manager;* Valerie Younkin, *Desktop Publishing Specialist*

PAPERBACK ISBN: 978-1-4166-1484-5   ASCD product #113003   n2/13

Also available as an e-book (see Books in Print for the ISBNs).

Quantity discounts: 10–49 copies, 10%; 50+ copies, 15%; for 1,000 or more copies, call 800-933-2723, ext. 5634, or 703-575-5634. For desk copies: www.ascd.org/deskcopy

Library of Congress Cataloging-in-Publication Data

James-Ward, Cheryl.

Using data to focus instructional improvement / Cheryl James-Ward, Douglas Fisher, Nancy Frey, and Diane Lapp.

pages cm

Includes bibliographical references and index.

ISBN 978-1-4166-1484-5 (pbk. : alk. paper) 1. Educational indicators—United States. 2. Education—United States--Statistics. 3. Educational evaluation—United States. 4. Effective teaching. 5. School improvement programs—United States. I. Title.

LB2846.J35 2013

371.2'07--dc23

2012037850

22 21 20 19 18 17 16 15 14 13   2 3 4 5 6 7 8 9 10 11 12

USING DATA
To Focus Instructional Improvement

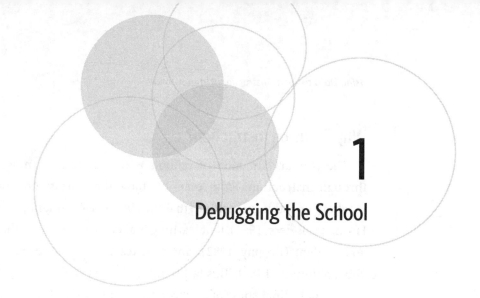

1

Debugging the School

How is it that some schools make progress and others do not? In other words, what do highly effective schools do that makes a difference? The answer is fairly obvious. Effective schools use information that is available to them to continuously improve. Those improvements might be related to the culture of the school, the cleanliness of the facility, or the instructional program. The data—information—focus the efforts of the staff members on areas of strength and need.

The problem is not that some schools have access to information and others do not. Schools are awash in information about most aspects of their operation. Some schools just choose to ignore the information that is available to them. Other schools take a look at the information, perhaps take the time to acknowledge the problem, and then do nothing further about it. And still other schools examine the data, develop an intervention plan, and then fail to implement or monitor the plan. This book examines schools that function differently—schools that make a difference by using information available to them to continuously improve, specifically in the area of instruction. Starting with the assumption that opportunities for improvement always exist, we must purposefully seek out errors, understand their causes and effects, and then fix them for continuous improvement to occur. In the parlance of computer programmers, this process is called debugging. As such, continuous assessment can be used by virtually any educational system to study and then improve the experiences and outcomes of the people who teach and learn there. We are not saying that continuous instructional improvement is easy; we are saying that it is worth the effort.

Why Focus on Instruction?

The primary function of schools is to facilitate learning, which is accomplished through instruction. From years of study, the educational community knows quite a bit about effective instruction: that the climate can enhance or reduce learning (Wright, Horn, & Sanders, 1997), that learning is a reciprocal process that occurs between teacher and student (Brophy, 1982), and that teacher expertise matters (Darling-Hammond, 2000; Shulman, 1987). This last point has been made abundantly clear through a large-scale longitudinal study of the economic repercussions of access to high-quality teaching. Three economists (not educators) drew from two sources of data—federal income tax records and standardized test scores—from 1988 to 2009. These two data sets are readily available, but not commonly linked. The economists' ingenious approach? Investigating the economic impact of a high-value teacher (top 5 percent) on the lifetime earnings of a student. Their analysis revealed that having a high-value teacher for one year correlated with a $50,000 lifetime earnings increase for that student (Chetty, Friedman, & Rockoff, 2011). They further reported that these students were more likely to go to college, and that the girls were less likely to become teenage mothers. By definition, not every teacher can be in the top 5 percent; it is mathematically impossible. But the most encouraging news is that replacing a low-value teacher (bottom 5 percent) with an average one equated to overall lifetime earnings that approached $1.4 million dollars per class of 27 students.

The economists' study speaks well to the continuous investment that should be made on the quality of instruction. Increasing teacher expertise positively affects the quality of life for our students long after they have left our classrooms. Replacing a low-value teacher doesn't need to be swapping out one individual for another; "replacing" could mean effectively supporting each teacher's professional growth. What if the instructional skills of every teacher were increased? Consider the effect this change would have on students. Do you know any teachers who aren't eager to become more expert at what they do? If so, they are in the minority of your collegial group. As educators, we all desire to be better at our job today than we were a year ago. We want to hone our teaching skills. But after the first few years of practice, during which we work out the obvious kinks of classroom management, lesson planning, and organization, where do we turn?

Our answer is that a climate exists within a successful school where data analysis, both quantitative and qualitative, informs instructional expertise. In too many schools and districts, data analysis is viewed as something separate from the daily life of the class-room. In too many instances, data analysis is reserved for a professional development session or scheduled for professional learning community discussions. These events are finite, with a start and stop time, and are only fitfully carried into the classroom. The challenge, as we see it, is to view data—not intuition, not anecdotal reports—as the tools we use to get better at teaching students. To get better at teaching requires us to relentlessly focus our attention, with laser-like precision, on instructional practice and improvement.

Focusing on Instructional Improvement

The first three phases of the instructional improvement model we propose have a lot in common with other systems that have been developed (e.g., Bambrick-Santoyo, 2010). More specifically, any instructional improvement system should begin by *surveying the information available within a school*—both hard and soft data—which is the focus of Chapters 2 and 3. Collecting hard and soft data require that school teams and their leaders develop assessment literacy, meaning that they come to understand what the assessments do and do not measure as well as the validity and reliability of the collected information.

In addition, a systematic approach to instructional improvement requires that *data are analyzed to identify patterns of strength and need.* The vast amounts of data that are available can overwhelm school teams to the point that they become paralyzed in the analysis phase and are unable to use the analysis to move to action. We have found it important in this phase to take time to celebrate successes and achievements. Although instructional improvement is about continuous progress, taking time to recognize areas of growth builds the capacity of the teams while reinforcing the notion that their efforts are rewarded.

The third part of a traditional approach to instructional improvement focuses on using the insights that were highlighted through analysis to *develop goals and objectives* that can drive the school improvement process forward. In high-performing schools, teachers and leaders engage as a community in all three phases of this process, from data collection to analysis and goal development. Developing specific and shared goals helps focus the efforts of a school and guides decisions about professional development and spending priorities, ensuring that there is significant community stakeholder involvement and investment in the outcomes.

Unfortunately, at this point in the process, many instructional improvement efforts end. In some situations, school teams meet at the beginning of the year, review their data from the previous year, and develop goals based on observed patterns. Then the school year starts and the well-meaning adults within these systems become busy as they do their best to meet the goals, but are unable to continue to assess the success of the implementation in all areas that affect students, faculty, staff, administration, and curriculum. The situation could be worse. Imagine a school where the principal independently analyzes data and then announces the goals for the year to the faculty and staff. Or worse yet, the leadership team receives information from the state assessments and files it away in a drawer, meaning to look at it later.

Despite good intentions, it's no wonder that some schools fail to improve. Instructional improvement is not the sole responsibility of the principal or even the leadership team. It is a shared responsibility of all the school's stakeholders, including students, parents, community members, classified staff, faculty, and administrators. It's also not about the plan itself. Simply writing goals and objectives for school improvement and sending the list to the district office or state department of education will not likely change the experience students have in school.

Following a Process

Developing an improvement plan is vital and will be addressed in more detail in the coming chapters. Let's temporarily put that to the side so we can highlight what happens *after* the plan is developed. Most conventional plans acknowledge that implementation and monitoring are important, yet offer few details on how that might be accomplished. Some teams assume that, once crafted, the details of the plan will fall into place. But then the inevitable occurs—competing priorities overwhelm the best of intentions and the plan is derailed. We contend that implementation and monitoring are all about building, maintaining, and extending the competence and confidence of everyone involved. And to do so, administrators need to see themselves as learners and to understand what it means to be a learner.

When it comes to developing our own students' competence and confidence, we turn to a gradual release of responsibility instructional framework (Fisher & Frey, 2008a). The framework is informed by the reading comprehension work of Pearson and Gallagher (1983) who provided a means for describing the shifting levels of cognitive responsibility between teacher and student as the learner gains knowledge and skills. Our own work has further expanded this view by including other vital aspects of instruction, including setting purpose and fostering collaboration among peers. Concepts and skills are introduced to students through focus lessons that include statements of purpose as well as modeling, demonstrating, and thinking aloud by the teacher. The cognitive responsibility shifts a bit toward students during guided instruction, when they get an opportunity to apply the skill or concept under the watchful gaze of the teacher, who is available to help when understanding breaks down. Students use these skills and concepts in collaborative learning arrangements, where vital opportunities to make mistakes are paramount. As competence and confidence grow, the student is able to assume an increasing level of cognitive responsibility to learn independently and continue building knowledge. Figure 1.1 contains a diagram showing the shifting cognitive and metacognitive responsibility at each phase of learning.

FIGURE 1.1
Gradual Release of Responsibility Instructional Framework

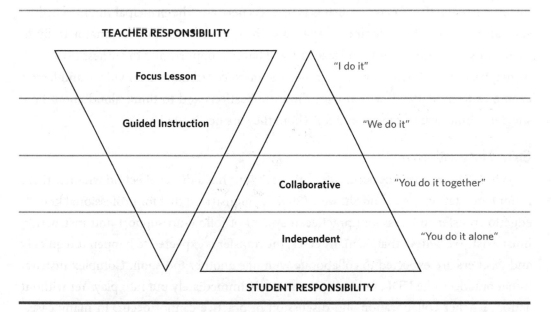

Source: Fisher, D., & Frey, N. (2008). *Better learning through structured teaching: A framework for the gradual release of responsibility* (p. 4). Alexandria, VA: ASCD. Used with permission.

The same principles for learning apply to adults. Our collective competence and confidence require the same kinds of scaffolds and supports. As with a classroom instructional framework, these concepts and skills rarely roll out neatly in a single lesson but are built over many lessons that occur over days, weeks, and even years. One notable difference in this instructional frame when we are teaching and learning with K–12 students versus when we apply it to support work with a faculty team is that the roles of "teacher" and "student" are not so clear cut. Within the context of instructional improvement, the "teacher" may be an instructional leader, the reading coach, or the 5th grade team, and the "student" may be the instructional leader, the reading coach, or the 5th grade team. Depending on what is being taught and learned, the roles should shift fluidly. We'll look at each phase of the gradual release of responsibility through the lens of instructional improvement.

The focus lesson

Purpose is established for the group, driven by the data or the need for the data, and it is essential for stakeholders to know exactly what is being done and why. For example, a school might analyze data and determine that mathematics achievement among students with special needs has stalled. An agreed purpose might be that the mathematics teachers need to learn more about the principles and application of universal design for learning (UDL). To accomplish this, the teachers and the principal might schedule several professional development sessions with the district math coordinator to build their skills. In these sessions, the teachers will have an opportunity to witness how UDL principles are used within the discipline. The math coordinator uses videos and lesson examples to model and demonstrate these applications and to think aloud about how she determines when, where, and for whom they are best suited.

Guided instruction

What does or does not occur after focus sessions has a direct effect on whether there is implementation. Joyce and Showers (2002) demonstrated that for professional knowledge to transfer to classroom practice, a system of follow-up support and instruction must exist. We believe that, in many cases, the transfer is expected to happen too quickly and teachers are expected to collaborate with one another too soon. Complex instructional practices like UDL, for example, are rarely immediately put into play. Yet without action, teacher collaboration and discussion of practice cannot occur. In many cases, what needs to happen after the initial focus lesson is some guided instruction. Guided instruction occurs when small groups of learners try out newly learned skills with an expert analyzing their learning using questions, prompts, and cues (Fisher & Frey, 2010b). In the instructional improvement process, guided instruction might include work sessions with a team of teachers.

For example, the primary and intermediate grade teachers who participated in the initial professional development sessions with the district math coordinator decided to break into smaller groups to work with the special educators assigned to their grade bands. K–2 general education teachers worked together to analyze their math curricula to identify possible areas to improve using UDL principles, while the special educators for each grade level guided their understanding. During the work session, one of the special educators recognized that several math teachers possessed the misconception that one UDL accommodation alone would meet the needs of all students with special needs. She used questions, prompts, and cues to draw their attention to what they knew about individual students. The general educators soon realized that because of their students' diverse needs, more than one accommodation would be necessary to realize the UDL principle of making information perceptible.

Collaborative learning

In this phase, learners work together to refine their collective understanding of a concept or skill. Collaboration is essential to learning because it is the phase where errors can and should occur on a regular basis. Errors are critical to the learning process, as they illuminate what we know and still don't fully understand. This phase also primes learners for subsequent instruction, as they become more attuned to locating information to fix errors. In the case of the primary math team, they tried out the materials they had created using UDL principles in their own classrooms and then met in their professional learning community to report on their progress and areas of difficulty. During the course of their discussion, teachers brought examples of student work to analyze together. Teachers found that most of the targeted students had performed better than expected using the materials, but they also discovered that in two cases the students performed worse. The team members suspected that although they had designed and implemented the UDL accommodations adequately, they did not agree on the underlying mathematical concept they were teaching and consequently testing. Confounded by these findings, the teachers invited the school's math coach to do some follow-up guided instruction with them on the finer points of using mathematical models to explain concepts.

Independent learning

Learning is always iterative, in that it always moves forward and serves as a gateway to new inquiry. Our march toward learner independence is so that the learners we are charged with teaching can resolve problems outside the classroom. Similarly, in a continuous instructional improvement process, educators are increasingly able and willing to apply concepts and skills to new situations over time. But to do so, they need to have a sense of competence and confidence, also known as self-efficacy. For instance, 1st grade teacher Kim Larson discovered that she had a talent for and interest in using UDL principles and began to use these as a lens for looking at her curriculum. In time she attended several webinars and conference sessions on universal design for learning. After reading a book on UDL, *Teaching Every Child in the Digital Age* (Rose, Meyer, Strangman, & Rappolt, 2002), Ms. Larson used an online tool to analyze curriculum for barriers as part of the professional development for teachers new to their school (see http://www.cast.org/teachingeverystudent/tools/curriculumbarriers.cfm). By combining her experiences with learning about UDL and applying these principles in her own classroom, Ms. Larson has evolved from being strictly a learner to facilitating the learning of others. In the next section, we will look more closely at how a middle school has woven the processes of gathering and analyzing data with those that focus on professional development cycles to foster continuous instructional improvement.

Instructional Improvement in Action

The faculty and staff of Mountain View Middle School met in late August to review student performance data. This school educates more than 1,000 students in grades 6–8, with 62 percent of the students qualifying for free lunch and 35 percent classified as English language learners. Within three years, the students at Mountain View made considerable progress. The achievement gap was closing, and students were performing at higher levels than ever before. The school attributes the gains to a systematic instructional improvement effort that starts with regular reviews of data and the development of goals and objectives that drive its curriculum and professional development work.

At the start of the school's data review session, the facilitator invites faculty and staff to a campfire—a metaphor for the interactions they will have with one another. The room is arranged in a circle of chairs, with tables and materials pushed to the outer perimeter. Faculty and staff are invited to share their celebrations, news, and greetings from the summer. The facilitator of this meeting is the mathematics department chair, Marc Rose. In other meetings, different faculty and staff members have served as the facilitator. Mr. Rose reminds participants that it's impossible to drive by looking only in the rearview mirror, and that the purpose of data is best served when it is used to determine where to go next. Following a 20-minute campfire conversation, Mr. Rose transitions the conversation to the purpose of their work at that time: understanding and analyzing the data, formulating the right questions, and figuring out the next steps. Two questions are posted on chart paper on the wall:

- What do we know from the previous school year's data?
- How does this information compare to prior years?

Participants are invited to walk around the room and discuss the data charts. These visual displays of data will be added to the data room at school and will remain on the walls as a reminder for at least the next three years. Groups of five to six people (across content areas and grade levels) view the data charts and write questions about the data they are reviewing on sticky notes and affix them to the charts. Some of the questions that are asked include:

- Why did 6th grade have the lowest math scores?
- What changed to ensure that writing conventions improved consistently over the past three years?
- How can we maintain our 96 percent attendance rate?
- How do we attribute the decline in suspensions?

[handwritten margin note:] ask about outliers

As they finished the carousel walk of posted data charts, participants were invited to return to the campfire to debrief. Each participant was provided a copy of the data and individuals were invited to share and explain what they noticed from a quick review of the data. The questions from the charts were then used to guide the debriefing.

The carousel and debriefing process required about an hour. In the past, this process took longer mainly because participants were not accustomed to looking at data, and some people became defensive about the implications of the data. Although no specific names were attached to the data, grade levels and subjects were identified. The principal had worked hard during the past couple of years to ensure that instructional improvement was viewed as a supportive process that resulted in celebrations and accomplishments.

At this point in the meeting, Mr. Rose invited participants to share celebrations relating to the data and everyone laughed, clapped, and passed around snacks. The range of celebrations from this meeting is noteworthy as many of the participants included information about past areas of focus in their comments. For example, Brenda Smith (a clerical staff member) said, "We've really maintained our attendance. Remember when these meetings focused on getting our students to school? Now, look at us! They're here, and it makes that part of my job easier so that I can get to some other things that need to get done."

Building on Ms. Smith's comment, Spanish teacher James Jimenez added, "And when they're here, they're learning a lot more. Just look at writing conventions. That was our focus last year. We all said that we would integrate a little bit of this into our content areas, and look what we did. We more than met the goal."

The celebratory conversation continued for several more minutes, with accolades for specific staff members and students. Mr. Rose then turned the group's attention to the next step—pattern analysis. In groups of four or five, participants were invited to brainstorm questions about the patterns they were noticing and to write these questions on chart paper. Groups were given 10 minutes to brainstorm and record ideas and were then asked to choose the three most important questions to share with the whole group. English teacher Debbie Fadol recorded the questions on a large chart. When all the questions were listed, people were asked what they noticed as a result of this exercise. They were reminded not to jump to conclusions or solutions, but rather to focus on the trends across the questions.

Cathy Lancaster, a 7th grade social studies teacher, focused on the achievement in mathematics saying, "We've come a long way and made a lot of progress. But I think it's time we tackle something that is a bit harder for us all: math. I've even said to my students, 'I'm not so good in math' and referred them to the after-school program and faculty for help. Last year we took on writing conventions, and we all agreed to do that. In retrospect, that was easy. It's time to focus on math, which means that we're all going to need to learn some math so that we can help our students. I know that this sounds strange coming from me, but if I learn the math itself, I'll figure out a way for students to practice in my social studies classes."

Mr. Rose asked for comments, all of which supported Ms. Lancaster's proposal to focus on math and the need to continue the work on writing conventions. Bob Villarino, science department chair, added, "We look at data all year long. And we use our formative assessments to guide what we do with individual students. But I agree with Cathy. We should make math our big push for this year. Let's drill down and see what we can do."

During the next phase of their conversation, teachers looked at item analysis reports on mathematics. In reviewing the math data, two specific strands were identified because of the low percentage of successful students. Both the measurement/geometry and the statistics/probability strands were areas of noted deficiency. These two areas account for 33 percent of the test, so they have a significant affect on student achievement. As groups of teachers reviewed individual student test scores, they began to notice that there was a significant population of students that scored proficient in nearly all strands of the math test with the exception of two strands: geometry and statistics. As they continued investigating the data and looking for patterns, Ms. Lancaster interrupted the groups, excitedly announcing, "These students are all within one to five questions from moving into the next proficiency level. That means we could really change this trend with some attention to the issue. And, we can all focus on statistics in our classes. I can easily do that in social studies, and so can a lot of other teachers. I would like to learn a bit more about this to be sure that I'm teaching it right, but I'm excited. This is way more doable than I first thought."

Within this meeting, staff and faculty agreed to goals and objectives, including:

• Goal: Students at Mountain View Middle School will improve their math scores in statistics/probability and measurement/geometry.

» Objective 1: The target intervention group will increase scores on the measurement/geometry strand of the math test to 65 percent by the end of the school year.

» Objective 2: The target intervention group will increase scores on the statistics strand of the math test to 75 percent by the end of the school year.

» Objective 3: The target intervention group will score 80 percent or higher on the specified strands of the benchmark tests that are given every four weeks.

» Objective 4: The target intervention group will score at least 8 out of 10 on weekly measurement/geometry and statistics quizzes that will include content and academic vocabulary.

In some school systems, this conversation and the identification of these targets would be seen as significant progress. And they are. In other schools, a discussion about data and the development of a target group for systematic intervention simply does not, or cannot, happen, and that type of environment is not sufficient to improve instruction. Our goal in this text is to share strategies for developing and implementing systems that allow for continuous improvement of instruction.

Thankfully, the staff and faculty of Mountain View Middle School understood that their data review and analysis along with the development of goals and objectives were just the first steps. As part of their discussion, they also identified the learning that would need to occur if they were going to meet the objectives. They also understood that they needed to focus on the curriculum, and not just in the math classes, to accomplish these goals. The staff and faculty acknowledged the tension that exists in adding something to the curriculum while trying to maintain momentum on the previous years' goals. They scheduled additional assessments to review later in the year, and they planned quick, focused observations in classrooms, also called learning walks or walk throughs. In other words, they knew that the success of their school improvement would be an ongoing process, not a single event.

During a subsequent meeting, the county math coordinator gave a presentation to the entire staff. The purpose of the professional development event was posted on the wall: "To expand our collective understanding of statistics such that we can integrate statistics practice in lessons at least weekly." The visitor modeled several lessons from different content areas and showed a video clip from an art class in which students were asked to calculate statistics from survey results they had collected from patrons at a local museum. The presenter paused the video several times to think aloud about the process the teacher was using and to name the procedures that were helpful in building student learning.

During the week that followed the professional development event, teachers met in their course-alike groups with the principal and district curriculum coordinator. The principal said, "It's hard on my calendar to be in each of these meetings, but I need to learn from this process and I need to ask the right questions as I guide this process." In the course-alike meetings, groups of teachers considered the effect of the additional focus on statistics on their pacing guides. They were not provided an answer, but were guided in thinking about how to address the goal and objectives that they developed at the start of the year.

In addition, teachers met in their professional learning communities to look at data that included the math benchmarks as well as data about student performance in their own classes. These meetings were not routinely attended by site administrators. Each group maintained notes about the meeting so that the group members could look back on their discussions. As teachers collaborated with their colleagues, they consolidated their understanding and planned interventions for students who were not making progress. Individually, teachers implemented their curriculum, developed and used formative assessments to gauge student understanding, and were observed by their principal and various walk-through teams.

Quality Assurance

As we stated at the beginning of this chapter, an underlying assumption of continuous instructional improvement is that problems exist and are not readily apparent to the user. Our job as educators is to seek them out, analyze them, and find a way to address them. Some problems are surprisingly easy to fix, but most are not. In fact, the ones that are most entrenched can be the most difficult to address, precisely because they have become part of the fabric of the school. Exposing these problems, examining them closely, and fixing them can extend over many months and years. The time commitment alone demands that there be a process for gauging progress. This process, called quality assurance, is "the planned and systematic activities implemented in a quality system so that quality requirements for a product or service will be fulfilled" (ASQ, 2012). In an organization as complex as a school, monitoring the processes related to instructional improvement is crucial because it is so easy to become consumed with daily demands and lose sight of the longer view.

We will end each chapter of this book with a section called quality assurance. This section is meant to serve as a reminder to do the parallel work of ensuring that there is a means for making the kinds of mid-course adjustments that will necessarily occur, without losing sight of the goals your school set out to achieve. In this first chapter we discussed the components of a gradual release of responsibility instructional framework, and its application to adult learning in schools with faculties that strive for continuous instructional improvement. We concluded with a description of one middle school as the staff members located and identified a problem, and then charged themselves with the task of fixing it. Before reading the next chapter, please take some time to reflect on the following questions designed to debug your school:

- What is the history of instructional improvement at your school or district?
- What efforts and initiatives have worked well? Why do you believe that is so?

- What efforts and initiatives have failed? Why do you believe that is so?
- What lessons should be carried forward as your school or district engages in continuous instructional improvement?

2

Taking a Hard Look at Hard Data

Challenge: Principals, how do you expose your faculty and staff to data on a daily basis?

Most of us have structured our daily lives to remind ourselves of the things we should do. We hang a motivating photograph on the refrigerator door to prompt us to make healthy food choices. We keep a packed gym bag in our car to cue us to work out at the end of the day. We place hand sanitizer dispensers in strategic locations so we remember to use it at warranted times. These subtle messages are called nudges, and they can be incorporated into the environment to nudge ourselves and others into making good choices (Thaler & Sunstein, 2008). An entire field of study called behavioral economics examines how environments can be engineered to guide people to make safe, healthy, and environmentally conscious decisions. For example, rumble strips on the road encourage you to slow down and signal when you are drifting out of your lane. Painted footsteps on the sidewalk lead you to a trashcan to throw away your litter. Lunch rooms are structured so that you must walk past the salad bar before selecting less healthy food items.

At the high school where three of us—Doug, Nancy, and Diane—work, we use hard data as a nudge. Although many schools have developed rooms for displaying testing results and attendance figures, access is usually limited to teachers and administrators. We realized that our data analysis could be used more effectively if we increased the number of people who view it. Therefore, four years of test score and high school exit exam data are displayed on the cafeteria walls above the food service areas so that students can view these results. The data are charted so that students can follow their graduating

] Data in staff lounge

Data in cafeteria... att daily

15

class's progress from freshman to senior year. Each mathematics teacher conducts occasional classes in the cafeteria to use the data charts in novel ways to teach principles of algebra and statistics to her students. At the top of the main staircase, daily attendance data are posted for each grade level, as well as the monthly averages. When 11th grade's attendance dipped midyear, the teachers met with students to discuss the issue and made plans to increase support for stressed students.

In the context of education, data are any information that we can glean about teaching and learning. To improve schools, educators must consistently use data to determine where they are and what needs to be done next. For data to be effective, they must be widely available and be used to affect instructional and policy changes. As we stated in the previous chapter, we need to view data analysis at its point of use: the teaching and learning that occurs in the classroom, in front of students.

In this chapter, we will focus our attention on hard data—how the data can be quantified, disaggregated, and most important, leveraged to nudge the changes needed for continuous instructional improvement. It's all about becoming "choice architect[s] ... [who have] the responsibility for organizing the context in which people make decisions" (Thaler & Sunstein, 2008, p. 3).

Hard Data Defined

Hard data are quantifiable; hard data can be described with a given degree of specificity and tangibility. In addition, hard data are relatively stable in that they aren't changed significantly by the method in which they are collected. The most common form of hard data generated for schools is derived from student assessment results. Other readily available hard data include attendance, suspension rates, and teacher credentialing. Hard data are gathered by some form of counting, and most hard data come from official or organizational sources. A difference between hard data and soft data is in collection and analysis. Hard data are usually converted into numbers and displayed as graphs. Soft data are displayed using qualitative methods such as anecdotes, testimonials, and quotes that reflect patterns and trends. Both are actionable and should be viewed as complementary. The soft data of an individual student's story breathe life into the numbers. Likewise, the hard data of attendance affirm the difference between an isolated incident and a noteworthy trend.

Hard data are reported using descriptive statistics that answer three questions: *Who? What? When?* The following statements are examples of how hard data are reported.

- Thirty-seven percent of the students in 4th grade scored proficient or advanced on the algebra and functions strand of the state content standards exam in the spring.
- Seventy-eight percent of 5th grade boys scored 340 points or higher on the math section of the second district benchmark assessment.
- Fifty-two percent of 2nd graders scored proficient in written conventions on the grade level writing rubric in May.
- Fourteen percent of 9th grade students missed five or more days of school during the first quarter of the school year.

These data can be collected using teacher-based, criterion-based, or norm-referenced assessments, and can be formative or summative in nature. However, if the reports of data are limited to snapshots of achievement, they fail to illuminate a pathway of improvement. For this reason, we advocate that comparative statistical analyses are also used to determine trends. These answer a fourth question: *Compared with what?*

- Thirty-seven percent of the students in 4th grade scored proficient or advanced on the algebra and functions strand of the state content standards exam in the spring, which is a 3 percent increase for this cohort over last year's performance in 3rd grade.
- Seventy-eight percent of 5th grade boys scored 340 points or higher on the math section of the second district benchmark assessment. On the first benchmark, 66 percent of these students scored in this range.
- Fifty-two percent of 2nd graders scored proficient in written conventions on the grade level writing rubric in May, compared with 49 percent in March.
- Fourteen percent of 9th grade students missed five or more days of school during the first quarter of the school year. Last year, 19 percent of freshmen missed five or more days in the same quarter.

The comparative use of hard data lets us know what interventions are working and to what extent. It can also alert us to possible problems that are slowly taking root, or serve as an early warning that a previously effective intervention may need to be reevaluated. However, numbers alone don't tell the full story, and they are easily misused if assessment literacy is lacking.

Being Assessment Literate in Hard Data

We often discuss issues of literacy for our students, but we rarely apply the same conditions to our own learning. We don't mean the educational definition of literacy, which relates to reading, writing, speaking, listening, and viewing, but rather its root: *literate*. Consider the synonyms of the term: *educated, scholarly, knowledgeable*. Similarly, assessment literacy is being educated about the instruments, scholarly in analysis, and knowledgeable in interpretation. Assessment literacy "comprises two skills: first is the ability to gather dependable and quality information about student achievement; second is the ability to use that information effectively to maximize student achievement" (Stiggins, 2001, p. 20). An essential part of being assessment literate is in understanding how, and under what circumstances, data are collected. Given that the most common type of hard data used for school improvement comes from state and local assessments, let's take a closer look at norm-referenced and criterion-referenced tests.

Norm- and Criterion-Referenced Tests

Most commercially prepared tests fall into one of two categories: norm-referenced and criterion-referenced. Normed tests are used to compare the performance of an individual student with others across a larger population, usually a national one. Tests of intelligence such as the Weschler Intelligence Test for Children yield an intelligence quotient for test takers. Some achievement tests, including the Iowa Test of Basic Skills or the Stanford Achievement Test, provide similar rank ordering, and generate the familiar bell curve. Results are typically reported as percentiles, with further analyses such as stanines, which scales the test results into nine segments. Because the purpose of an IQ test is to compare participants using a bell curve, the instrument is designed so that the majority of students score near the middle. Although norm-referenced testing has some applications to education (like intelligence testing), it is of limited value when measuring the learning of students. For this reason, most standards-based tests are criterion referenced.

Criterion-referenced tests are assessments created to determine student mastery of content. In other words, they tell us to what degree a student has learned something. A teacher-created assessment on stoichiometry for her chemistry students is a criterion-referenced test, because it gives the teacher and her students information about how much they learned during this unit of instruction. Likewise, the district-created science benchmark and the state standards assessment for chemistry are criterion based. In each case, a student's level of proficiency is reported along cut points, or predetermined scores that convert quantitative measures into performance bands. The cut points for a unit test on stoichiometry are reported as grades, whereas the science benchmark is likely to have cut points tied to identified bands of mastery or lack thereof such as *intensive, strategic, basic, proficient,* or *advanced.* Students in the intensive and strategic bands are said to be in the most need of intervention. Those in the proficient and advanced bands are deemed to have mastered the tested skills. The state chemistry standards test provides students, as well as their families and schools, with information about how the individual performed and often gives similar cut point information.

Using Criterion-Referenced Tests for School Improvement

At the *federal level,* hard data are collected annually about elementary and middle school student performance in the areas of reading, writing, and math; and about high school student performance in the areas of reading, math, science, and world history via the National Assessment of Educational Progress (NAEP). These assessments are administered to 4th, 8th, and 12th grade students in schools across the country and are proctored by NAEP personnel. Student results from these criterion-referenced tests are disaggregated to compare academic progress from state to state. Often called "the nation's report card," NAEP scores are not reported at the individual student level. Instead, these results are used to formulate policy and determine funding.

At the *state level,* hard data are collected annually from every school in every district beginning at 2nd or 3rd grade. Schools administer state standards-based assessments within a timeframe tied to the number of days students have been in school; that is, students in every school take the test after being in school for the same number of days. Students are assessed in the areas of language arts, math, science, and social science. Districts and schools across the state compare student results broadly by subject area and also drill down to examine the results by content cluster and strand. Unlike NAEP, the results are tied to individual students, making it possible for schools to identify those in need of intervention the following school year. A compelling purpose for developing the Common Core State Standards was so that results could be compared across states as well as within, because portions of the testing instruments will be identical.

At the *district level,* hard data are collected several times annually through criterion-referenced benchmark assessments. These tests are usually administered to every student in specific grades at the end of each quarter or trimester. Information from the district tests are used at the district level to gauge progress, compare schools, and identify schools that might need assistance. Data that are generated include the number and percent of students scoring at or above a given cut score in each content area. The data are further analyzed to determine students' progress toward outcome standards. These district tests are administered and analyzed to provide timely interventions to students to bolster learning.

At the *school level*, similar common formative assessments are collected on a more frequent basis to improve the precision of teaching and intervention. These criterion-referenced assessments provide information about progress and are further used strategically to ensure that student performance information informs future decisions.

Looking Deeper

Of course, schools are not one-dimensional, and achievement data do not fully portray the nuances of school life. Other readily available hard data are used to describe the students in a school. Demographic data are reported across many attributes, including race, ethnicity, gender, disability, and socioeconomic status. In addition, home language surveys are collected and analyzed to identify English learners. How these demographic data are reported and disaggregated is regulated according to federal and state guidelines. The purpose of these demographic data should go beyond mere description and be further analyzed to allow schools to look deeper for students who might otherwise be lost in the data deluge.

With the enactment of No Child Left Behind (NCLB), schools were required to pay attention to the achievement of all students. Schools and districts now report the performance of students by subgroups: black or African American, American Indian or Alaska Native, Asian, Filipino, Hispanic or Latino, Native Hawaiian or Pacific Islander, white, two or more races, socioeconomically disadvantaged, English learners, and students with disabilities. By disaggregating state results by subgroups, the federal government forced states to examine the achievement of all groups of students.

But you may recall an earlier time when students with identified disabilities were tucked into the corners of high-performing schools. Their numbers alone were usually not enough to affect the overall achievement of an entire school, as they typically composed only 8 to 15 percent of the student body. It was simply a byproduct of the mathematics of achievement. A school with a high overall level of achievement wasn't going to experience sufficiently depressed scores to warrant attention. Students with disabilities were always there, hidden in plain sight. But the accountability measures required by

NCLB changed that. Although the NCLB accountability measures remain controversial, most educators agree that the measures illuminated an overlooked portion of our school population. More than a decade later, it is hard to imagine achievement discussions that don't include students with special needs.

Attendance data provide another lens for examining the pulse of the school. Most educators are familiar with applying attendance data at the individual level to alert us to those students whose chronic absenteeism places them at risk. But absence rates can also be used to locate patterns among students. For example, by examining school health records, demographic information, and absence rates, a school may find a significant relationship—perhaps that habitually absent black students have poorly controlled asthma. Asthma is the most common chronic illness of childhood, and poor, urban black boys have the condition at a rate 45 percent higher than the rate for peers (Basch, 2011). What initially may have been perceived as a motivation issue may be a health one, and the solution is to coordinate family, school, and community supports. In this case, the health issue warrants having asthma action plans for students, reducing environmental triggers at school that can set off an attack, and creating a case management system for students whose asthma is severe and poorly controlled (Basch, 2011). Identifying effective health interventions for these students, rather than behavioral interventions, would not be detected as a possible solution without the know-how to look beyond standard data reports to mine information *across* reports.

A third commonly reported statistic relates to suspension and expulsion. Since the 1970s, many studies have clearly demonstrated that American Indian, Latino, and African American students are disproportionally suspended or expelled from school (Gregory, Skiba, & Noguera, 2010). Despite efforts to reduce this disparity, it persists. Causes have been proposed, including poverty, environmental and cultural attributes that differ from school, and higher rates of selection for formal discipline in school and the justice system. But one factor that is often overlooked is achievement. Low literacy achievement is often viewed as a product of high rates of disciplinary action, but more rarely recognized as an opportunity for intervention. For instance, Miles and Stipek (2006) reported that low literacy levels in the primary grades predicted aggression in 3rd grade. And though it is common for elementary schools to design and implement early literacy interventions, it is less common to look at discipline rates among participants in the literacy programs. Yet both the achievement and the behavioral data are already there, just waiting for someone to look at them together. That's just what a team of researchers

literacy
intervention
studies...
discipline
vs
literacy

did with kindergarten students at risk for literacy failure. The researchers coupled a literacy intervention with positive behavior supports and found improvements on both measures (Volpe, Young, Piana, & Zaslofsky, 2012). By viewing both achievement and nonacademic hard data together, surprising relationships can come to light. And with that insight can come some very good ideas about what to do about it.

Demographic information about students, as well as nonacademic data such as attendance and discipline rates, can help us look deeper into the corners to address the needs of learners that we might not recognize as harbingers of patterns or trends. In addition, the ways we use hard data can herald a growing problem that we have overlooked. The ability to spot trends requires using the data both formatively and summatively.

Using Hard Data Formatively and Summatively

Hard data can be analyzed to inform or to summarize. Hard data are considered summative when used to describe the results of a process and formative when used to inform and adjust processes as they unfold. Summative assessments tell us how well students, schools, or districts did at the end of a given period of time. Teachers use summative data in their classrooms to determine students' unit, semester, and end-of-course grades. Similarly, schools and districts use hard data summatively when reporting annual growth or proficiency status. These summative analyses of hard data are used to rank states, districts, schools, and even groups of students.

A summative view of hard data is not without limitations, particularly because it gives us only a look at what has already occurred. Reeves (2005) compares summative data to an autopsy, where the patient is already dead and now it's a matter of determining what killed him. On the other hand, formative assessments are akin to physical examinations, "an uncomfortable ordeal, but… preferable to and less intrusive than autopsies" (p. 53). An important detail inferred in this analogy is that formative data should not become mini-autopsies. In the same way that you would be dismayed if your doctor didn't discuss the results of your physical to recommend healthy changes to your diet and lifestyle, so should you be if colleagues are only using formative data to evaluate, but not to make changes. You can't fatten pigs by weighing them (Jones, Carr, & Ataya, 2007). Formative use of hard data should inform us so that we can make thoughtful adjustments to maximize results.

Nonacademic data such as attendance, office referral, and suspension rates are not generally regarded as formative, but they should be. As we described at the beginning of this chapter, these data can be analyzed for trends and patterns. If there are outlier class periods, subject matter, or times of day when attendance either significantly spikes or decreases, data can be further analyzed to inform instruction and other school programs. Referrals are often overlooked in terms of informing instruction; however, if students are routinely removed from certain classes for behavior reasons then school leaders must not only examine student behavior but also classroom environment, environmental fit, and teacher preparedness. Much like referrals, suspension data can give us information about instruction. Unfortunately, when the instruction does not meet the needs of the students or if the instruction fails to acknowledge the contributions of all students, then they may become disengaged or even disruptive.

Likewise, demographic data should be reviewed each year to determine shifts in student subgroups and are imperative for improving instructional strategies and curriculum. Although demographic information is relatively stable from one year to the next, there are exceptions. For instance, after Hurricane Katrina devastated southern Louisiana and Mississippi in 2005, some school districts found themselves hosting significant numbers of traumatized children and families. They experienced a sudden onset of students who needed significant academic and psychological supports. An analysis of middle and high school students who fled the destruction found that the students who did best were those who transferred to schools that "created a milieu of cooperation... and neither went overboard trying to help nor ignored their special needs" (Barrett, Ausbrooks, & Martinez-Cosio, 2012, p. 7). Without question, these schools looked closely and frequently at their data to achieve this careful balance.

In addition to guiding how we modify or improve instruction and intervention, formative applications of hard data provide feedback to groups or individuals. A good feedback system clarifies the goals and is specific and descriptive of the work and its progress (Varlas, 2012). Assessment measures that can be used to provide feedback include baseline assessments, progress monitoring data, and benchmark assessments. Nonacademic hard data that can be used to inform instruction include attendance, referrals, and suspensions by class or period, teacher, school, or district. For example, a high school tracked tardy slips and office referrals over a two-year period as it switched to a later start time and found a significant reduction in both. The hard data were persuasive feedback for families and community members who had opposed the change to a later start time and were doubtful that it would be effective.

It has become common practice to gather frequent monitoring data to determine student progress toward a predetermined set of goals, especially through a response to instruction and intervention process (Fisher & Frey, 2010a). These data often include a record of reading fluency scores or timed mathematics calculations. In practice, however, these formative assessments are unidirectional; that is, they are used to view student progress, but more rarely to evaluate instruction. Thus, a student's lack of progress is described just that way—it is the *student's* failure. But formative use of hard data must also be used to assess the effectiveness of the instruction. Using a formative lens, the record or log not only gauges student progress over very short periods of time but also becomes a tool for determining how instruction should be refined. Using the record is much like using the diagnostic data used in the medical profession to identify specific areas of need. With this information, a treatment plan is prescribed and monitored. A failure of treatment is seen as just that—it is not a failure of the patient, but rather that the treatment needs to be adjusted. Our teaching should be understood the same way, but it requires us to be willing to look at hard data as a mirror of our instruction, and not simply as a description of the inevitable (Dimmock & Walker, 2005). The use of data to inform instruction has proven to be a boon to students and teachers. Black and Wiliam's (1998) review of the formative use of data to improve instruction stated that the achievement gains associated with it are "among the largest ever reported for educational interventions" (p. 61).

In the same way that we use formative assessments to determine what should occur next in the instructional cycle, so should formative hard data be used to inform what should occur next in the school improvement cycle. A decline in absence rates merits a closer examination of what is proving to be effective for improving school attendance. A rise in disciplinary referrals should prompt further investigation into root causes.

Making the Data Useful

Schools that are successful—and know why they are—use achievement and nonacademic data throughout the year to guide and refine instructional practices, programs, and student placement. They pay attention to achievement by subgroups and use formative assessments to address the needs of each student. When state assessment results are published in late summer, these schools have no surprises. Results can be predicted within a few data points. These successful schools use assessments to triangulate their findings; moreover, in such schools the process of using hard and soft data to inform instruction is cyclical.

Triangulation is the use of three or more data sources to arrive or converge on the same findings. It is a means of determining targeted information from multiple data sets. For an architect, triangulation means discerning with precision key load factors and points in space and time from other reliable and predictable data (White, 2011). If themes or findings are established by converging several sources of data, then the process of triangulating data sources adds to the validity of the findings (Creswell, 2008).

Steps to Inform Instructional Improvement

We provide a step-by-step process to make data useful in informing instruction. These steps can be used to transform ideas into action.

Start early. Data teams, leadership teams, and school leaders start the process of looking at school data at the beginning of each school year. But schools that use data to improve instruction don't stop there. They continue to review both hard and soft data throughout the year, paying close attention to everything from progress monitoring reports to quarterly benchmarks, and from classroom observations to annual state standards tests. The overall goal is to improve instruction by closely monitoring achievement results, nonacademic indicators, and classroom practices. Highly effective schools use both hard and soft data to refine programs, design teacher supports, and respond to intervention needs.

Look for links between practice and results. Identifying contributing factors that increase student achievement starts at the beginning of the school year. The instructional data team should analyze schoolwide state test results to determine how the school, grades, content areas, subgroups, and individual students performed. It can compare the results with the state assessments from the previous year. The team will then begin to ask questions about overall growth. Were there changes by subgroup, by grade? Were there content clusters that were outliers because the results were comparatively high or low? If so, the data team can review the previous year's formative assessment data to see whether the summative results could have been predicted earlier. Keep in mind Reeves's (2005) caution to avoid turning a data review into an autopsy. If the only outcome is to identify indicators, but no action is taken, then one shouldn't expect the future to be much different from the past. The team's goal is to find changes and consider their causes in order to develop an action plan.

Expect the unexpected. If the results from the initial analysis are unexpected, the data team might then review and compare the alignment of formative and summative assessment measures. Use the additional data to calibrate the type of data the team is collecting and analyzing to see if they are in fact the right measures. The more aligned the state assessment is to district benchmark assessments, as well as teacher-created measures, the more accurately these predictors can inform practice.

Make the findings public and encourage speculation. The data team next presents these findings to the entire school and its stakeholders, including families and students, for further discussion. The data team displays the data in a way that is comprehensible and encourages discussion about other plausible reasons for the outcomes. Information is presented in the form of texts, tables, charts, and graphs to paint a picture of the results. (We will discuss visual displays of data in Chapter 4.) The format selected to present each piece of information should be carefully considered to ensure ease of understanding and to highlight key data. The same information is also presented in different ways to provide an analysis through various lenses:

- Schoolwide by content area and grade
- By content area, grade, and subgroup
- By content area and subgroup
- By content area, grade, and gender
- By content area and gender
- By content area, grade, gender, and language proficiency levels
- By cohort bands, content area, and proficiency levels
- By test year, content area, and subgroup
- By test year, content area, and grade
- By test year, content area, and gender

Drill deeper to examine classroom data. At the beginning of the school year, teachers should analyze their prior year state test results and end-of-year summative assessment to determine their own teaching strengths and challenges. By reviewing content subcluster areas for their prior year's students, teachers can determine where their instruction was effective and where it needs to grow or change. Strong content subcluster area results are one indicator of effective instruction, but do not stand alone. Teachers should review these subcluster results along with classroom observations and nonacademic data to glean information about student performance as well as to self-assess their performance.

Anticipate the needs of new students. Rearview data from the previous year can be further leveraged to identify the needs of incoming students. Teachers should expect to have state standards assessment results for their new students to determine where needs might be. It is especially important to be proactive by identifying students who have already amassed a record of academic or social struggle. No child should have to wait until the first reporting period is over before being noticed as a struggling student. It is much easier to begin the year with anticipated personal, curricular, or technological supports in place than to try to make up lost ground after 25 percent of the school year is over. Teachers across a grade level or discipline can meet to look for larger patterns and trends to identify whether more intensive supports are warranted. For example, in our school, the 11th grade team matched incoming students' test results from the previous year to locate students who needed coordinated academic support. Traditionally these hard data would have remained at the individual teacher level, and the chemistry teacher would not have realized until much later that a struggling student was also having trouble in math. Instead, the grade level team identified 24 students in need of academic support before the school year even began. The team was able to build the students' schedules so they could access the school's academic recovery resources from the first day.

At the elementary school where Cheryl was principal, grade level teams of teachers met at the beginning of the school year to analyze state test data. Students who scored in the Below Basic and Far Below Basic range on the California Content Standards tests were identified for diagnostic assessments in an effort to identify their specific areas of need. Students were then clustered in fluid groups by need for intervention during the school day, and in some cases had additional intervention time before or after school. The specific information from the test was also used for unit planning to determine when to slow down instruction and when to increase the pace.

Pay close attention to historically underserved subgroups. Analyzing state assessment data by subgroups helps to ensure that students who may have been historically overlooked receive instruction that meets their needs. Districts, schools, and individual teachers must examine the content delivered, the method of delivery, and the cultural proficiency of those delivering the instruction (Lindsey, Robins, & Terrell, 2009). This point about subgroups was brought to our attention by the 9th grade team members, who were concerned that advanced students were not being sufficiently challenged. They identified specific students and assigned each student a mentor teacher from their team. Throughout the year, they met regularly with identified students to hold academic discussions. Word about these mentoring meetings soon got out, and the 9th grade team began hosting "power lunches" that were open to all students. These power lunches featured guest speakers from various professions. Although the individual mentoring meetings still continued, the intervention for advanced students broadened to meet the interests of a wide array of students.

Plan regularly scheduled dates to analyze interval data. After the first benchmarks are administered, the data team will reconvene to analyze the new hard data and to develop charts, tables, and graphs to share the data with the rest of the staff. Once again, the team will analyze these data across content areas, grades, subgroups, cohorts, teachers, and gender. The results will be compared to state test results and the previous year's first benchmark results to gauge growth over time. This process will again be repeated at the end of the second and third benchmarks with more information being added for discussion.

Instructional Improvement in Action

Whether they are new to a school site or returning for their tenth year, principals begin by querying the data. They must analyze their students' results from both state and local assessments. Principals have to analyze data for trends and patterns in student outcomes to determine academic strengths and weaknesses. In addition, they review classroom observation data and outcomes from learning walks, requiring an in-depth exploration of the connection between instruction and student performance. To ensure that the information is correct, they triangulate it with other data sets to ensure accuracy.

For example, Principal Mario Marcos begins a new elementary school assignment in early August, when the state test scores are just released. He reviews those scores along with the end-of-year district course assessments. In his district, students take summative assessments in math, writing, and reading to determine student growth over the school year. Mr. Marcos also consults the attendance records, reviews suspension and expulsion rates, and reads the classroom observations that had been conducted by the former principal.

Mr. Marcos knows that an isolated review of the data is inadequate to his school's needs and that the data team is a rich resource, especially to someone new to the school.

The data team can offer the context of the last school year, especially as it relates to the school's goals and its ongoing professional development. He invites the team to meet with him to learn about the data together. Mr. Marcos posts questions around the room to guide their exploration of the numbers.

- How did students do overall in math, reading, and writing?
- Were there specific strands that ran across all grade levels in which students were notably strong or weak?
- Are there patterns we see across subgroups?

Mr. Marcos and the data team begin to plug in the numbers on chart paper in order to see if any patterns are emerging. After posting the state standards-based test results with the district end-of-course data, they compare the two. One member of the team remarks, "According to the district assessment, we performed well in math, but that's not what the state test results say." A discussion of possible explanations ensues, and Mr. Marcos listens carefully. At this early stage of analysis, he is aware that data teams often want to move prematurely to solutions. "Those are interesting possibilities," he says, "but let's keep digging."

He and the team examine additional hard data. They view last year's suspension and expulsion rates, and though they find them to be low compared to the district average, they are the highest they have been in five years. "That's really disturbing," another data team member observed. "I wonder what happened last year?" Mr. Marcos reinforces her question. "That's a great question, and that's the point of this data dig. We want to pull the questions to the surface." He adds her question to another chart labeled "Questioning Our Data." As he writes he says, "We've got two now. 'Why are there discrepancies in math performance between our state test results and those on the district assessment?' And the second is, 'What caused our suspension and expulsion rate to rise so much last year?' We'll use these questions to guide our next steps." By the end of the morning, Mr. Marcos and the data team have reviewed student performance data, nonacademic measures, and last year's professional development goals. In addition, they have generated six questions and are beginning to see that it's too early to propose solutions. "We just don't have enough information yet," a team member reasoned. "We need to look at the soft data, too." Mr. Marcos smiled and said, "Let's have lunch first, then we'll take that on this afternoon."

Quality Assurance

Throughout this chapter we have discussed the types of hard data that are available to administrators and data teams. The data that come to mind first have to do with student achievement, especially on state standards-based tests. Although these provide necessary information, they are limited in scope as they highlight only one aspect of student performance. Other hard data include safe schools reports, attendance records, suspension and expulsion incidences, and even health records. Another limitation is the way in which hard data are conventionally used. They are most often a look backward at what has already occurred. It is informative to know where you have been. But in the same way that you can't drive a car by only looking in the rearview mirror, you can't steer a school toward improvement by only looking at last year's results. These data are made more useful when they are examined for trends and compared to data across several years. In addition, hard data are often right under our noses, waiting for us to spot them. Other than end-of-year assessments, assessments can be analyzed formatively throughout the school year to make timely adjustments and to design new interventions. In all cases, the goal is to make data results widely available to stakeholders who can nudge students, educators, and families toward action. As you review the hard data results at your school, keep these quality assurance questions in mind:

- What do the achievement results report?
- Are these achievement results consistent across subgroups?
- Are there subgroups who are underserved?
- What nonacademic data are available to us?
- Are we examining the hard data at regular intervals?
- Are we examining the hard data across reports as well as within?
- Do our observations result in action?

3

Using Soft Data to Bring Information into Focus

In 1854 during a cholera outbreak in London, John Snow, one of the fathers of epidemiology (the study of the incidence and prevalence of disease) attempted to solve the mystery of the disease with quantitative tools. The prevailing theory suggested that cholera was caused by pollution or bad air. Given the conditions of London at the time, that explanation was reasonable. But Snow didn't believe air was the origin and posed the possibility of infected water as the culprit. At first, his quantitative analysis of the water did not conclusively prove its danger (at least with the chemical and microscopic analysis tools he had available). Undeterred, he talked with people who lived in a specific area that had a high incidence of cholera. Going door-to-door and interviewing residents, he identified a water pump on Broad Street as the source of the outbreak (Hempel, 2007).

The qualitative analysis of data was enough to convince the local authorities to disable the pump, despite the fact that germ theory was not yet understood. Snow's analysis and the resulting actions of the local council are credited with ending the cholera outbreak. Snow then created a spot map to illustrate the clustering of cholera cases around the location of the pump and used statistics to determine the relationship between the water source and cholera cases. Snow noted that the Southwark and Vauxhall Waterworks Company, using water from sewage-polluted sections of the Thames River, was delivering the water to some locations via pumps, leading to an increased incidence of cholera. Researchers later discovered that the public well had been dug only three feet from an old cesspit, which had begun to leak fecal bacteria into the water supply (Johnson, 2006).

So what does this story have to do with instructional improvement of schools in the 21st century? It's a reminder that we need to collect soft or qualitative data by observing and interacting with the people being studied or involved with a study. Hard or quantifiable data can tell part of the story, an important part to be sure. But getting behind the data to determine what's going on, to counter a prevailing theory, or to identify root causes require access to soft or qualitative data. As we discussed in Chapter 2, it's important to remember that quantitative or hard data can mask identification of groups of students in need of intervention. Other times, the hard data highlight priorities. In both cases, qualitative data can help clarify the problem and guide intervention efforts. In addition, soft data can be used to monitor progress of the goals that are established to improve the instructional program.

Soft Data Defined

Soft or qualitative data refer to information about student learning and instruction that is acquired by observing student and adult actions in and out of classrooms. It can include information about the classroom environment, instructional support, and use of instructional strategies. Unlike hard data, soft data are all around us. Rather than being found on paper, on the shelves in offices, in data binders, or in electronic files, soft data are uncovered in classrooms, staff lounges, main offices, playgrounds, athletic fields, and in the corners of the school. It is part of the realm of qualitative inquiry (Merriam, 2002), which is rich in description of people and their actions, behaviors, and discussions. Qualitative inquiry provides a myriad of ways to examine learning, and the end result of qualitative inquiry is soft data.

How soft data are gathered is very important. Hard data sources are primarily official organizational statistics, but soft data reflect the underlying currents of a place or situation that can easily go unnoticed precisely because they are so ubiquitous. As an old saying goes, "The last thing a fish notices is water." The qualitative research tools for gathering soft data include surveys, interviews, opinion polls, and observations. With each of these instruments, the intent is to shine a light on an element of a school's daily life.

Learning occurs through the academic and social interactions of teachers and students, and the hard data of test and attendance scores cannot adequately capture this information. Therefore, gathering soft data is focused on listening to the language and interactions between and among students and staff, analyzing the details of teaching and learning, and examining the culture and climate of the school. Soft data are described in words and pictures rather than numbers and convey what the observer has learned (Merriam, 2002).

Hard data give us a snapshot in time and describe how students are doing but not necessarily why. Soft data put a human face on the numbers. Using both soft and hard data, school leaders, data teams, and individual teachers can determine what is working well and what is not, and then begin to explore the causes. By thoroughly examining processes throughout the school—classrooms, school culture, outdoor spaces, offices, and meeting areas—root causes for student achievement or lack thereof can be specifically identified. Unsuccessful processes can be modified, adjusted, or eliminated and successful ones replicated.

Triangulating both the hard and soft data sets around a single process allows educators to get a precise picture along with a detailed written description of the events leading up to or surrounding the picture. Without the soft data, we have a picture but few if any details about why the picture is occurring. The triangulation of both hard and soft data around a focal point completes the picture, one that teachers and data team members can use for discussion of next steps. Although soft data may appear on the surface to be fuzzy, in truth they increase the precision of school improvement efforts. Hard data alone cannot reveal the important nuances of a school's successes and challenges. Soft data, when combined with hard data, bring both of these into focus.

Being Assessment-Literate with Soft Data

As with hard data, the quality of soft data is directly proportional to the expertise of those who gather and interpret the data. When collecting soft data, it is essential to understand the influence of sampling techniques, confounding variables, and instrument design on the quality of the soft data.

Know your samples. You've seen them in shopping malls. A swarm of eager poll takers equipped with clipboards invite shoppers to take a few minutes to complete a survey or to participate in a focus group. Some shoppers wave them off while others stop to fill out a form. Although this technique may appear somewhat haphazard, the research company is using a time-honored technique—volume. Researchers know that the risk of a small sample is in skewing the findings. For example, one grumpy and opinionated shopper can disproportionately influence the results of a survey totaling only five participants. But in a sample of 100 shoppers, the other 99 balance his views. Although the product in question may warrant his negative comments, a large sample size will tell you whether others share his opinion. In this case, the smartest guy in the room *is* the room. Likewise, when gathering data at your school, avoid reducing the number of participants to a meaningless size and don't handpick your participants in advance to favor an outcome you hope to find. For instance, asking the members of the school's football team if they think the athletic program makes a positive contribution is going to yield predictable results. Asking a large sample including both athletes and nonathletes will provide a more accurate picture.

But let's say you have a different question, such as whether the school's athletic program is helping or hindering student-athletes in their academic endeavors. This time you *are* purposefully sampling a specific group of participants. It wouldn't make much sense for students who are not in organized sports to respond to this question. The questions should lead you to the sample population you need. The opinions and insights needed for describing a school's collective viewpoint on a topic demand a large randomized sample. Those questions that target the experiences of a specific group require a purposeful sample of the group.

Know your confounding variables. Many outside factors can get in the way of the questions we seek to answer through soft data. For instance, it's probably not a good idea to conduct a school climate survey on the Friday before winter break, because you're likely to get unusually high marks. On the other hand, we wouldn't administer this survey in the middle of midterms, when students are feeling more anxious than usual. Choosing an ordinary day in January is going to give you credible findings. Better yet, a series of four climate surveys spread across the school year will provide trend data. These factors, called confounding variables, can include the timing, gender, ability, experience, or other factors that directly or indirectly influence the findings. Identifying possible confounding variables is important because they can provide vital explanations of the results. To use a non-school example, both ice cream consumption and murder rates rise in the summer. But eating ice cream doesn't cause murders, and those touched by a murderous event don't eat ice cream to make themselves feel better. Rather, there is a confounding variable at play here—the weather. In the summer, more people are outdoors in the sweltering heat and eat ice cream to stay cool. They are also in contact with more people outdoors than in the winter, when people tend to stay home. All that contact can have dangerous outcomes, but it doesn't have anything to do with how much ice cream is eaten. Awareness of confounding variables, such as the timing of your survey, can contextualize results and prevent false conclusions.

Know your instruments. Soft data are collected using a variety of research tools that should align with the questions you are seeking to answer. A question about family participation and attitudes toward school will likely require an anonymous survey so you can collect lots of information from a broad audience in an efficient manner. You may want to explore the question further by comparing and contrasting the experiences of families who volunteer at school with those who rarely visit school; in this case, by inviting representative samples of parents from both groups to participate in focus groups. Conducted in a friendly environment participants are asked a series of prepared questions, or probes, to ensure that their discussions are parallel. Because the school itself may be a confounding variable, focus groups could be held at a neutral site, such as a local community center.

In other cases, the information you are seeking may be of a sensitive or complex nature and may warrant individual interviews. Your question may revolve around the school's effectiveness in responding to bullying. Delving into the experiences of victims, perpetrators, bystanders, and interveners requires a delicate approach, and gathering them together into one large room is not going to result in productive conversation. Instead, a caring adult should conduct these conversations using an individual interview process. As with focus groups, a protocol of questions should be prepared to ensure parallelism.

Another tool for gathering soft data is observation. Unlike tools discussed previously, observation tools do not require direct contact with the person being observed. Observations may be simple tallies, such as the amount of time it takes for all the students to be in their classrooms after lunch is over. At the other extreme, observations can be quite complex and require the input of many to design a proper instrument, such as a classroom observation form. Most, however, fall somewhere in the middle range. In all cases, observations should reflect the nature of the questions being asked, and should be piloted to make adjustments to the design. From surveys to focus groups, from individual interviews to observational tools, all should align to the questions being asked. More complex questions, such as those surrounding school culture and climate, may require multiple instruments.

Examining the Culture and Climate of the School

Every school has a culture and a climate. To examine school culture, there must first be a clear understanding of the concept of culture. Schein (1992) defines culture as "a pattern of shared basic assumptions that a group learned as it solved problems of external adaptation and integration, that has worked well enough to be considered valid and therefore to be taught to new members as the correct way to perceive, think, and feel in relation to those problems" (p. 12). Deal and Kennedy (1982) define culture as "the way we do things around here" (p. 4). Bolman and Deal (2008) further state that culture as a product "embodies wisdom accumulated from experience. As a process, it is renewed and re-created as newcomers learn the old ways and eventually become teachers themselves" (p. 269).

School climate is about the feel you get when walking onto the campus. Climate refers to how students and teachers interact with and among one another (Lindsey et al., 2009). It is the feeling one gets being on the playground, in the office, and in individual classrooms. You can visit several 5th grade classrooms and the climate may vary from room to room, but the overall feeling one gets from the school is called the climate (Harrison, 1992).

Schools attempt to capture their culture and climate through their mission or vision statements and core beliefs. These documents tend to be posted in the main office, data rooms, public areas of the school, on school websites and letterhead, as well as in teacher and student handbooks. Yet these documents tell us very little about the school culture or climate. The real description of a school's vision, culture, and climate is determined by the way in which school personnel interact with each other and students, the way students interact with one another and school personnel, and the manner in which the inner school community interfaces and communicates with the outer community (Crowson, 2003). Moreover, school culture and climate are determined by student placement in general education, remedial, advanced, and enrichment courses, as well as by student involvement in after-school clubs and athletic programs. It is manifested in the school curriculum, disciplinary records disaggregated by subgroups, and home-school correspondence (Fiore, 2011).

Most schools' mission statements purport to help *all* students become productive citizens of the 21st century and to create caring, nurturing environments in which *all* students are provided with a number of opportunities to reach their full potential in a global society. When we analyze the placement data for students, we begin to get a sense of the real picture. At the secondary level, qualitative inquiry can be used to gather soft data from observation notes of counselor and student interactions. By analyzing the student placement by subgroups, soft data can be generated about the adults' beliefs regarding students' abilities. If large numbers of minority students are placed in remedial courses or if disproportionately fewer minority students are enrolled in advanced placement courses, that action serves as a manifestation of unstated core beliefs. Similarly, if few girls are enrolled in science, math, or advanced placement courses, that is an indication of core beliefs. Looking further at the hard data regarding placement in enrichment courses or special programs provides us with direction about the soft data we need to gather.

Principals in two middle schools of different sizes collected soft data to determine if their schools were fulfilling their mission. At Principal Monroe's middle school with 700 students, the mission statement professed providing the social and academic skills, environment, and support needed for each student to reach his full potential in a family setting where every student was valued for being unique. Yet placements of student subgroups that encompassed 40 percent of the student population were void in language enrichment courses. Special writing courses offered before school inadvertently excluded bused students who arrived too late for these sessions. Worse yet, when Mr. Monroe observed a media class, he noticed that students were separated by ethnicity and that one group of students was allowed to use the equipment but the other was required to work in a separate area of the classroom on written assignments. The soft data told Mr. Monroe a great deal about the school culture, which was quite different from that claimed in the school's mission statement.

Soft data from Principal Bradley's 1,200 middle schoolers revealed a different picture. The mission statement asserted that all students shall be surrounded and taught by caring adults who continuously participate in professional growth in order to understand how to provide every student with a rigorous and relevant education in a supportive environment that ensures the success of all. When Ms. Bradley walks into a science class, she finds the teacher beginning the lesson with a discussion about an African American astronaut and nuclear physicist. The teacher draws parallels to the physicist's work and the new unit of learning. Ms. Bradley notes that the student composition of the class matches that of the school demographics. As she reviews the bus schedule, she notes that there are five late buses for students who remain after school to participate in various enrichment and athletic programs. These soft data reveal a school living up to its mission statement, which proclaims an inclusive and celebratory culture.

At Mr. Monroe's school, fights on the quad often occur across ethnic lines and sub-groups—these groups generally don't intermingle. This separation is also displayed in classrooms in which students sit in clusters by ethnicity. He notes that adults also separate themselves along ethnic lines. The soft data reveal that the school misses the mark on *valuing the uniqueness of every student in a family environment* as reported in its mission statement.

Ms. Bradley reviews the number of suspensions for the quarter and finds only two for the entire period. She decides that this low number is a good sign for a middle school of 1,200 students. As she begins to ponder why, she notes the teacher professional development calendar, the student positive discipline calendar, and the character-building program that the school adopted four years ago. Ms. Bradley notes that professional development and student assemblies are scheduled monthly, not one of them has been canceled since she arrived at the school three years ago. These soft data lead Ms. Bradley to believe that the school is espousing its mission statement.

Soft data about school culture and climate can be obtained from correspondence. If a school has a large number of second language learners and the correspondences are sent in the most widely spoken student languages, these soft data provide evidence about the willingness of the school personnel to communicate with all parents. If the school is socioeconomically diverse and school information is sent home only by e-mail, these soft data yield a different finding about the school culture and climate (Fiore, 2011).

"When examining school culture and climate it is important to remember that they are not stagnate, but rather dynamic entities that may change. Both influence and are influenced by the behaviors, values, and practices of the school" (Lindsey et al., 2009, p. 125). By observing the practices for student placement, instruction, retention, disciplinary issues, and parent communication, you can learn much about both the culture and climate of a school. Like hard data, soft data can be formative and used to make schoolwide changes in culture.

Looking in the Corners

The front office and staff lounge are important components of the school and can be excellent sources of soft data. The transactions in both of these areas of a campus are climate trendsetters and have significant implications for student learning. Each area provides a wealth of information regarding school culture, climate, school-community relations, student-teacher interactions, and the schoolwide learning environment.

The front office is like the welcoming committee that greets a delegation at the airport. It is the hospitality suite and the concierge, and is where most parents, students, and the larger community get their first impression of the school. If the individuals in the front office are too busy to welcome their clients, it communicates that other matters are more important than human presence (Crowson, 2003).

A data team wanting to learn more about the many aspects of student learning could obtain a great deal of data from the front office. Questions that members seek to find answers to might include: How do the personnel in the front office greet individuals? How long does it take for a person at the counter to be greeted? Are different ethnic groups treated differently? If so, how? How are students treated when they come to the front office? Are the front office personnel helpful in getting students and adults where they need to go? Do they attempt to answer all questions or to find the answers to those questions they cannot answer themselves? Do they treat parents and students with respect? How do front office personnel answer the phone? Do they respond to district calls differently than outside ones? If so, how? Where is the office entrance? Can front office personnel immediately see and greet individuals from where they sit? How is the office furniture arranged? Is it closed or opened? Is the office tidy and clean? Is the mission statement posted? What do students think about the front office? What do parents think about the front office? What do teachers think about the front office?

The data team can use qualitative inquiry to answer these questions, observing front office transactions and noting exactly what occurs. The team then sifts through its notes seeking emerging themes or common occurrences. With these soft data the team is ready to make some suppositions about the school culture and mission. Moreover, the team can add this information to the hard data gathered to get a clearer picture of the overall school learning community. For example, when Mr. Monroe walked into the front office of his school for the first time, he was surprised that no one acknowledged him. He was more surprised that the person behind the counter who finally did ask if she could help him, did so without looking up. Mr. Monroe, new to the school, then went to his office and began logging his soft data.

To find out more about the school culture, core beliefs, educational values, common practices, instruction, and the professional learning community, the data team might decide to camp out in the staff lounge because an abundance of data can be uncovered there. If the conversations in the lounge are mostly about sharing lessons and ideas, it might be an indication of a learning community where there is trust and collaboration.

If, on the other hand, most of the conversations are about how difficult students and parents are, that information provides a different, but important, piece of soft data. If teachers in the lounge sit according to ethnic groups rather than by department or grade, the data team will have found another important piece of information. The team may also want to know the feel or tone of the conversations—the climate of the lounge. General questions might simply be: How do teachers use their time in the lounge? What do they talk about? Answers to these questions can inform student learning, school culture, and climate.

Acknowledging the importance of gathering soft data, Principal Monroe decided to make it a point to eat in the staff lounge at least twice weekly. He hoped to learn more about the heart and soul of the school and get to know his staff on a more personal level.

Listening to the Language of Interactions

Listening to the language of interactions is about noting verbal communication between and among students and adults. It encompasses body language and facial expressions, both of which are culturally driven. Since many of our schools are ethnically diverse, an understanding of the cultures represented in the student body is also important. According to Dimmock and Walker (2005), "the reality of school life results from the complex interplay of cultural elements from society, region, and locality on the one hand and organizational culture on the other" (p. 25). Due to globalization and multiethnic communities, understanding the language of interactions of the ethnic groups represented in a school becomes that much more important.

Lindsey and colleagues (2009) assert that verbal interactions can fall into one of six categories, all of which have significant implications for student learning. When adult interactions and language seek to eliminate any culture other than the dominant one, that action is understood to be destructive. Verbal communication, looks, or cues that seek to dismiss the culture or contributions of subgroups are also destructive. Communication cues that trivialize or lead to the stereotyping of subgroups is labeled as culturally incapacitating and occurs when the language used by the dominant group seeks to make other cultures appear to be wrong or inferior to its own. When school personnel and students use language that ignores or seeks to ignore the experiences of individual subgroups or when communication cues seek to treat everyone exactly the same regardless of culture, then it is said to be culturally blind. Language transactions that show an intentional awareness of what someone knows or doesn't know about subgroups is said to be culturally precompetent. Communication that is inclusive of other cultures that are different from the dominant culture is said to be culturally competent. Finally, language that seeks to create social justice is said to be culturally proficient (Lindsey et al., 2009).

School leaders, data teams, and teachers wishing for instructional improvement cannot overlook the language of interactions. Teachers can gather soft data about their own interactions by watching video of their instruction or by asking colleagues or school leaders to script portions of their lessons. Examining video or scripted notes with administrators, peers, or students will add rich data that the teacher can use to improve instruction.

In addition to the data uncovered in the front office and staff lounge, data teams and administrators can gather a wealth of soft data from the verbal interactions across the campus: the halls during class changes, the playground, the athletic fields, the cafeteria, across the campus at dismissal and lunch, and within classrooms. Within classrooms, data gathering begins with the first interaction among students and adults. Teacher interaction includes eye contact, proximity, one-on-one instruction or lack thereof, small group instruction or lack thereof, whole group instruction, checking for understanding, teacher questions, prompts, verbal feedback, and praise of students' accomplishments (Los Angeles County Office of Education, 2000). The language of interaction also includes the number of times a teacher interacts with or possibly ignores individual students. Classroom data can be gathered via scripting and tallying interactions, taking notes, viewing videoclips, or listening to audiotapes.

The words used to usher students through the halls and into classrooms during class changes should be observed as well as verbal dealings among students. Similarly, the care with which adults and students communicate with and among themselves around the campus before school, during lunch, and after school can be revealing. Are the salutations enthusiastic, encouraging, remindful, and respectful or are they labored, rare, undignified, demeaning, or forced? Are language interactions between and among some groups of adults or students different? Are some adults or students treated differently? If so, how and why? Gather these data using appropriate observation tools.

The cafeteria and common eating areas are especially interesting because both socioeconomic and ethnic factors may come into play between and among adults and students. The climate in these areas is easy to detect. Gathering data in this case might include focus group interviews about where and when they eat and with whom.

Data teams and administrators can collect soft data on the playground and during school events via note taking and checklists. The team can begin with a set of questions or a hypothesis about language or a rubric of language interactions. If responding to open-ended questions, team members may want to write brief but descriptive notes about what they observe. If using rubrics, data teams and administrators might want to add a tally mark to a given column or range when certain language transactions are heard or observed. With note taking, the data are teased out by themes. Regardless of the approach, the team or administrator then reviews the data, possibly comparing the information to other soft and hard data for instructional decision-making purposes.

Collecting Teaching Observations

The single most important factor that affects student learning is instruction. What the teacher does in the classroom has a profound effect on students' learning (Leithwood, Louis, Anderson, & Walstrom, 2004). Therefore, the primary place to collect data on instruction is in the classroom. To determine the *why* behind hard data generated from student assessments, soft data must be collected from within the classroom walls.

Analyzing state assessment data at the beginning of the year sets the stage for collecting soft data via classroom observations. The hard data provide specific information on where to focus teacher observations or where to begin to look. After analyzing annual and quarterly hard data reports, principals, data teams, and teachers should pinpoint where to begin or shift the observation focus, perhaps focusing on particular content cluster areas, periods, grade levels, or teachers. Although there are targeted areas of focus, all teachers should be routinely visited. The principal and the support team must make daily visits into classrooms a primary goal.

Targeting specific areas should be a fluid process based on initial hard data and ongoing soft data acquired through classroom observations. If the hard data point to vocabulary development across the grades as a weakness, then teacher teams, instructional support staff, and the administrative team will want to visit classrooms with a focus on collecting data around the use of academic vocabulary. If the hard data point to 4th grade math as a starting point because math achievement is significantly lower in 4th grade than in both 3rd and 5th, then the instructional team will want to devise a plan for full observations in these classrooms. The principal, members of the instructional support team, or groups of teachers will observe lessons in 4th grade math classes to collect broad baseline data. After these data are collected, analysis begins. To determine why students are underperforming in one area as compared with others, the team will want to analyze and take notes in one or more of the following:

- Classroom environment, routines, and transitional structures
- Student understanding of the objective and lesson focus
- Teacher focus throughout the lesson
- Use of instructional routines for introducing new content
- Use of instructional routines to deepen student knowledge
- Verbal and posted celebrations of student work
- Evidence of prior instruction on the classroom walls
- Gradual release of responsibility
- Continuous checking for understanding
- Simultaneously engaging all students through pair share, cooperative groups, small group collaboration, or some combination
- Use of the 7:2 rule; no more than seven minutes of teacher talk for every two minutes of student talk
- Clear and focused closure for each component of the lesson

In top performing urban schools in the People's Republic of China, research indicates that most schools have open classrooms, meaning that teachers can observe colleagues teaching without notice. Teachers are required to observe at least one colleague daily and to provide specific feedback on instruction. Principals and curriculum specialists also spend time in classrooms daily and regularly provide specific feedback to teachers. In general, teacher observations should be conducted routinely by principals and the instructional support staff (Marzano, Waters, & McNulty, 2005) and as often as possible by fellow teachers (City, 2011).

We have found it helpful to focus classroom observations on specific aspects of the instruction. For example, observers at a school were looking for evidence of the connection between an established purpose and the group tasks that students were asked to accomplish. (See Figure 3.1 for an example of an observation). Of course, the soft data of teaching observations can, and should, be aggregated across classrooms to identify coaching, professional development, and collaboration time needs. These observations are not used for teacher evaluations but rather to inform the instructional improvement efforts of the school.

FIGURE 3.1
Teaching Observation Form

Teacher: Jessica Sanchez	Date: 1/6/12	Period: 2	Lesson Focus/Topic: World History

Teaching to:

- ☐ Individual
- ☐ Small Group
- ☐ Whole Class

- ☐ ELL
- ☐ IEP(s)
- ☐ Multicultural
- ☐ Other:

Notes: 34 students in the class; 4 students with IEPs

Establishing Purpose: (posted on board):

- Learn about the events and people of the Russian Revolution
- Examine the effects of the Russian Revolution on WWI
- Use our textbooks and smart phones to find historical information

Productive Group Work:

- When the teacher didn't get an answer on commonalities between the *U.S. Bill of Rights* and the *Declaration of the Rights of Man*, she said, "I want you to say hello to the people at your table, and talk with each other about what these two documents had in common." She visited three groups, then posed the question again to the class. This time, they were able to answer.

- Following her modeling while reading from the textbook, students were asked to compare the Glorious Revolution and the American Revolution by developing notes for the foldables in small groups. Each member was responsible for part of the note page and for contributing to the collaborative poster in writing.

Lesson Highlights

Students were working in groups of 4. Each group was constructing a conversation roundtable (good for group and individual accountability), and each student had a question to answer and teach the rest of the group. The questions were related to passages in the textbook (Background to the Revolution; Lenin and the Bolsheviks; Civil War in Russia; Triumph of the Communists). The teacher used a digital timer displayed on the board so students could gauge the elapsed time for their small group work.

   Students were fully engaged in the task, and there were numerous signs of joint attention (turning the textbook so a partner could see), as well as evidence of their learning (taking notes on the graphic organizer). As students worked, the teacher moved from group to group, sitting with each to facilitate discussion of the topic. At the end of the elapsed time, students were instructed to move to expert groups to more fully discuss a single question. Before moving, the teacher briefly revisited the purpose to reinforce why they had completed the task, and to set up the next portion of the lesson.

Summary

The pacing of this portion of the lesson was appropriate—there was no wasted instructional time, and the teacher instilled an appropriate sense of urgency in her students. She relied on a number of management techniques to do so (timer, questions on cards, graphic organizer, purpose and agenda posted on board). Beautifully organized, and students were actively working to deepen their understanding of the topic.

Copies distributed:

- ☐ Teacher
- ☐ Observer
- ☐ Other (specify)

Using Soft Data Formatively and Summatively

Like hard data, soft data can be analyzed to inform or to summarize. For example, the analysis of classroom observation data could be used to inform professional development efforts or it could be used to evaluate the effect of coaching efforts. The data collection process does not determine whether data are formative or summative; that's determined by how the data are used.

We discussed some of the challenges with summative, or autopsy, hard data reviews in Chapter 2. Many of those same challenges apply to soft data. We also talked about the need to use data formatively, which is also the case with soft data. The use of soft data, both summatively and formatively, can stir controversy as people might argue that the information is too subjective to be used in these ways. In most cases, however, if the data are collected using sound practices, the information will accurately represent some aspect of the school's operation.

For example, a vice principal interviewed 10 percent of the student body, randomly selected, asking students about ways to improve school attendance. About 50 percent of the students reported that they missed school on days when their favorite activities were not available. There were several categories of reasons, including illness and child care responsibilities. But that one category caught his attention. Several of the students said that they missed school when their chosen extracurricular activities were not available. Micah, as a case in point, said that he regularly missed Tuesdays because there's no basketball practice on Tuesdays and none of the other after-school options motivated him enough to go to school. Although these data could be dismissed as subjective, not related to student achievement, or based only on 10 percent of the students, they could be used to make adjustments to the offerings in the after-school program. In other words, these soft data could be used formatively.

As part of the interviews, the vice principal also asked about one of the efforts initiated the previous year, which was to post daily attendance rates by grade level. The majority of students indicated that posting the attendance rates was useful and that they understood that their lack of attendance would compromise the school's ability to meet one of its goals—to obtain 95.5 percent attendance for the year. These data were used as part of a summative review of efforts from the previous year.

Instructional Improvement in Action

Mario Marcos, the new elementary principal introduced in Chapter 2, is considering the soft data he and his team need to gather and analyze to answer the questions that surfaced through examination of the school's hard data. The first question concerned mathematics performance. When Mr. Marcos analyzed his end-of-year data with the data team, staff, and parents, they noticed that 3rd grade math scores were lower than those in 2nd and 4th grades. The team readily agreed that last year's 3rd grade cohort bears watching, and a member proposed doing some brief focus group interviews with students who scored at or above grade level, as well as those who scored below. In addition, the team decided that teacher surveys of mathematical instructional practices might be helpful. "Maybe there's a problem with alignment across these three grade levels," offered a team member. "The surveys can be anonymous, because our goal isn't to identify a single teacher. We want to look at their practices." Mr. Marcos noted, "That's a good idea. Let's pull data together and we'll decide where to go from there."

The team then turned its attention to the other question raised through the hard data review—a rise in the suspension and expulsion rate to the highest it had been in five years. "I'd like to take this one on," offered the school counselor. "I'll do individual interviews with the students and families of suspended students to find out how we handled these incidences." The team began brainstorming possible questions for an interview protocol that began to take shape. "That's going to help us put faces on the data," Mr. Marcos reminded the group. "The numbers alone can't tell us the full story."

Quality Assurance

We are surrounded by soft data but can fail to notice them unless prompted to do so. Like the air we breathe, soft data can become so much a part of our environment that we can be oblivious to them. An assumption of soft data collection is that we make a conscious effort to examine the information. Soft data sources include the interactions that occur in and out of classrooms, including the front office and cafeteria. The ways in which these soft data are gathered can have a profound influence on accuracy. Aligning our questions with the methods we use to gather information speaks to the level of sophistication of the data team. Poorly collected soft data yield faulty interpretation and ineffective intervention. As you review the soft data at your school, keep these quality assurance questions in mind:

- What do these soft data report?
- Do the soft data that we are collecting address the questions we are asking?
- Are we cognizant of the confounding variables that can interfere with our findings?
- Are these findings consistent across subgroups?
- Are there underrepresented or overrepresented subgroups?
- Are we examining the soft data at regular intervals?
- Are we examining the soft data across reports as well as within reports?
- Do our observations result in action?
- Are our soft data borne out by our hard data?

4

Getting to the Root of the Problem

Physician and writer Atul Gawande tells the story of a remarkable doctor and an obstinate teen. He describes Warren Warwick as a 76-year-old grandfatherly type and Janelle as a 17-year-old with "dyed-black hair to her shoulder blades, black Avril Lavigne eyeliner, four earrings in each ear, two more in an eyebrow, and a stud in her tongue" (Gawande, 2004). The one thing they had in common was cystic fibrosis—she had it, and he had devoted more than 40 years of work and study to developing effective treatment. At a regularly scheduled appointment, he noticed that her lung function had declined from 109 percent three months earlier to 90 percent that day—remarkably good for a CF patient. Most doctors would be pleased with these numbers, but Dr. Warwick was not. He asked her what was going on. Janelle replied in monosyllables that nothing was wrong. He persisted; she remained detached. Over the next several minutes, he was able to unearth the fact that Janelle had been skipping most of her twice-a-day percussive treatments and rarely took her medicine. He also learned that a new after-school job and a boyfriend were distracting her.

Dr. Warwick asked her to look at the numbers, explaining that the daily risk of getting a lung illness for someone with cystic fibrosis is 0.05 percent, and for those in treatment, it is 0.005 percent, a seemingly small margin. Multiplied across a year, he told his young patient, it "is the difference between an 83 percent chance of making it through 2004 without getting sick and only a 16 percent chance" (Gawande, 2004). In short order, he made a plan with Janelle. She would carry her medicine with her, even to class. Janelle protested that the medicine had to be locked in the school's health office. *"Don't tell them,"* he whispered. He called her best friend to recruit her in Janelle's daily treatment. His last decision was the one that made her cry—admitting her that day to the hospital to regain the lost lung function. She attempted to bargain with him. Could it be tomorrow? "We've failed, Janelle. It's important to acknowledge when we've failed" (Gawande, 2004).

Gawande asserts that excellence lies in these slim margins, and that knowing the difference between a 99.5 percent and a 99.95 percent success rate is what matters because lives are at stake. Gawande attributes Dr. Warwick's "focus, aggressiveness, and inventiveness" as explanation for his extraordinary success rate with CF patients—the highest in the country. His keen ability to notice apparently small changes, his relentless search for root causes of problems, and his alignment of interventions to address them place him at the top of his profession. Most important, his success means that his patients live longer, healthier lives than similarly diagnosed people who receive treatments at other facilities.

Although the work with our students isn't quite as life-and-death as Dr. Warwick's, it is nearly so. The daily work of school means that we administer to the academic, social, emotional, psychological, and physical health of children. Their daily success, or lack thereof, is compounded and magnified. Failure on one day might not mean much; failure every day portends the educational equivalent of death: another dropout. Indeed, an analysis of predictors for failing the California High School Exam revealed that the three strongest were grade point average, number of absences, and number of disciplinary actions. No surprise, right? Except that these predictors were evidenced in 4th grade, six years before the students actually took the test (Zau & Betts, 2008).

In this chapter, we will borrow a page from Dr. Warwick's playbook. We will discuss how noticing and identifying a problem using collected data alerts us to situations in need of our attention. Once identified, these problems need to be thoroughly explored using root cause analysis. And once we begin to understand what the root causes of the problem are, we can develop goals and objectives to reverse or eliminate it. By knowing that the slim margin between 99.5 percent and 99.95 percent makes all the difference in the lives of students, we can go from good to great.

Identifying the Problem

The collection of data, both hard and soft, is an essential first step in the school improvement process. Without data to examine, we are subject to impressions and anecdotal experiences, and decisions more closely resemble folklore than science. Many educators have worked in districts where the superintendent's newest initiative could be directly traced to the conference he attended the previous week. But in an era where "data-driven decision making" has replaced homespun knowledge, we face a different dilemma. The availability of data has been a blessing and a curse, with a fine line between swimming and drowning in data. Without a way to harness the data, we are no better off than when decisions were based on folklore.

Visual displays of data

In the previous chapters, we have examined hard and soft data and methods for collecting both types. Once collected, what can be done with the data? The short answer is that the data need to be displayed visually so a team can begin to understand how the results and findings relate to one another for patterns to emerge. However, we have all seen bad attempts at doing so. One bewildering graph after another can cause even the most dedicated educators to throw up their hands in frustration. To avoid this problem, it's useful to answer some questions about the data you have collected in order to determine how they might best be displayed.

- *Is the data quantitative or qualitative?* Quantitative data (numbers) are usually presented in graph form, and qualitative data (words) are best presented in table form. Types of graphs include bar, line, histogram, and pie charts.
- *How many data points need to be displayed?* A low number of data points (three or less) can usually be understood within a table, and greater numbers of data points are usually displayed as a graph. A bar chart is good for displaying data that are discrete, such as the yearly attendance by grade level each year. Histograms, which are similar to bar charts but touch one another, are good for displaying continuous data, such as the grade point averages of students enrolled in advanced placement courses.
- *How important are the relational frequencies?* Pie charts are the first choice for understanding how parts relate to a whole. For example, the percentage of students in a grade level who performed at the advanced, proficient, basic, and far below basic levels on the standards exam can best be understood using a pie chart.
- *How important are the trends?* Data gathered across multiple years are useful for determining whether the general trend is positive or negative. Line graphs can graphically represent a downward or upward trend. Bar charts with multiple years of data can

be a bit more difficult to interpret, but can be used to show many data points, such as performance by grade level for three years on the state mathematics test.

Many visual displays are generated through data management software programs that allow administrators to choose from an array of options. Keep in mind that the display should align to your purpose for the data, and should prompt analysis and not merely catalog the past. For this reason, all graphs and tables need to be clearly labeled and titled so they can be understood easily by educators as well as other audiences. The best data displays are accessible, both literally and figuratively, to all stakeholders. Therefore, data displays for elementary schools should include student-friendly versions that are developmentally appropriate. Schools located in communities where languages other than English are spoken should include data displays in home languages. Variations that address developmental and language needs communicate a powerful message of collaboration to students, families, and community partners. These displays also invite input beyond the designated data team and allow for different stakeholders to assume responsibility for action.

In keeping with this spirit, we also encourage schools to think closely about where the data are displayed. It has become popular for schools to designate data rooms for this purpose. However, these rooms are often located in places that require special admittance. We like to place data at points of contact, such as the front office, the cafeteria, and the top of a busy staircase. In our experience, we have benefited from the insights of students, families, and teachers who see the data each day. Their collective ability to detect patterns has triggered interesting conversations about what type of problem might be occurring, what are the possible causes, and how the problem might be addressed. Analyzing data is akin to watching the box scores of your favorite baseball team, and the immersion in an organization's data can lead to some innovative solutions. As with Dr. Warwick, inventiveness begins through close examination of available data.

Detecting patterns. A danger with the flood of school data is that it can quickly swamp the boat. Displays of data are an essential component, but without a process for examining them for patterns, the data themselves can become wallpaper. After the data have been compiled, we do a data walk with the school's team beginning with placing all the data on individual charts and hanging them around a large room. A facilitator is appointed who has been closely involved with data compilation. During this time period, members can get more information about the details of data and clarify their understanding.

After a period of questioning and discussion about the meaning of the displayed data, each member of the data team is given a stack of sticky notes. We ask members to write questions and observations, one per note. This activity is typically done individually; we don't forbid discussion with others, but we don't encourage it either. Members affix their notes on the appropriate chart, and the notes become the content for the next round of discussions. We reassemble around each chart, and the facilitator reads the questions and comments to the group. All the members participate in the discussion and provide useful insights into the details of the data. After each chart has been debriefed, the notes are removed from the chart and sorted on a blank wall according to similarities. Categories are not developed until after conceptually similar questions and observations are listed together. In most cases, five or six columns of notes are developed, and the group then collaborates on naming the categories. (We use a nearly identical process for the entire faculty and staff, but cluster participants gather in smaller groups to manage the discussions more effectively.) Although it takes more time and physical space to conduct a data walk, we find that process vastly superior to the conventional practice of reproducing data on handouts. Our intent is to encourage collaborative pattern analysis from the start, which is nearly impossible to do when the data are presented for individual consumption only.

Narrowing in on the problem. The categories developed by the team serve as an effective platform for launching the next part of the discussion: What are the problems we face? What are we doing well? It is vital at this point in the conversation to make sure that successes are not overlooked in the rush to name the problem. It's human nature to notice the troubles and dismiss the successes, in part because those successes are working and therefore aren't front and center. On the other hand, the possible problems are quite noticeable. The facilitator has two similarly named charts for capturing comments and insights about both problems and successes. She also reminds the group to temporarily refrain from identifying solutions (another human tendency) so that the group can stay focused on the immediate purpose. As each success and problem is proposed, the facilitator asks for evidence from the data. In addition, a series of questions are displayed to help the group think through the possible ways to examine the data. At times, the problems identified require obtaining more information about the data:

- Have we considered each significant subgroup?
- Have we considered each content area?

- Have we examined content clusters (for example, vocabulary within the English Language Arts portion of the state exam)?
- Do we detect upward or downward changes over multiple years?
- Are we adequately examining cohort data over multiple years?

Once problem statements have been drafted, we move into the next phase, which is hypothesizing possible root causes of the problems.

Examining Root Causes

Collecting and analyzing data to identify a problem is an important part of an instructional improvement effort, but is not sufficient. Simply identifying the problem and then developing goals and objectives to address the problem neglects an important part of the process, namely, the careful examination of the causes of the problem. Problems are best solved by attempting to address, correct, or eliminate *root causes*, as opposed to merely addressing the immediately obvious symptoms (Ammerman, 1998). To be effective, the root cause analysis should establish a sequence of events or timeline to understand the relationships among contributing factors, root cause(s), and the defined problem or event to prevent in the future. Root cause analysis can help to transform a reactive culture (one that reacts to problems) into a forward-looking system that solves problems before they occur or escalate. Preuss (2003) offers the following definition for root cause:

> **Root Cause**—the deepest underlying cause, or causes, of positive or negative symptoms within any process that, if dissolved, would result in elimination, or substantial reduction, of the symptom. (p. 3)

Supporting this definition, we find that highly effective school systems dig into their data to find deep underlying causes. Many times we identify several causes that deserve our attention, and finding the "deepest" cause can be challenging. For example, Olivia is failing all of her classes. One cause is her attendance, which stands at less than 50 percent. As a school system, we can attempt to do something about her attendance. We could also dig a little deeper into the cause of her poor attendance, which might reveal situations that we cannot address, such as chronic illness. Or it might reveal Olivia's responsibility to take care of a young sibling on days when her mom has to work, which we might be able address. In this case, we could argue that the *problem* in the school is low levels of achievement in a group of students, one *symptom* is failing classes, and one *cause* is attendance, which could be caused by a host of other factors. A cause is likely to be a root cause when:

- You run into a dead end asking what caused the proposed root cause.
- Everyone agrees upon the root cause.
- The cause makes sense and provides clarity to the problem.
- If the cause is addressed, there is realistic hope that the problem can be reduced or prevented in the future. (Croteau, 2010)

Identifying a root cause requires investigative skills, trusting relationships, and honesty. The leadership team must carefully consider each aspect of the organization to determine which factors are truly the cause of the problem that needs to be solved. The team members may need to interview stakeholders or reflect on their own practices. In some cases, the root causes are the "elephant in the room" that everyone knows exists but no one wants to talk about. In other cases, the root cause is hidden deep within the traditions of the organizations or may be a result of lack of awareness or information.

Components of an Educational Root Cause Analysis

The staff of the Center for Data-Driven Reform recommends the use of root cause analysis as an effective way to focus efforts (www.cddre.org). There are several components that teams must address if they are going to consider every aspect of the organization as suspect in contributing causes to the problem (see Figure 4.1). Although this approach sounds negative, we are reminded that the most effective systems in the world recognize that errors will occur and that these errors can be noticed and corrected. As we discussed in Chapter 1, it's really about debugging the school rather than casting shame and blame on the people who work in a given building. As an example of root cause analysis, we've included scenarios from Mountain View Middle School (from Chapter 1) as they discussed the need to improve their students' mathematical knowledge.

Student Factors

Many issues can be considered relative to the students who attend the school. Not all of these issues are under the control of the people who work at the school, but we see no harm in recognizing the realities that some students face and the skills that they bring as a result of their experiences, culture, or heritage. In discussing root causes, some of the student factors that might be appropriate to consider include attendance, measures of poverty, ranges of disability, number of languages spoken, maturity, interests, and motivation. The faculty of Mountain View Middle School identified *lack of test stamina*, *self-efficacy issues*, and *decreasing motivation as a result of poor test scores* as some root causes related to student factors. One of the teachers said, "I think we can include test stamina here as a student factor, but it also could have been put in the instruction category. We don't need to get into what to do about it now, we just need to know that it's part of the problem."

FIGURE 4.1
Common Root Causes

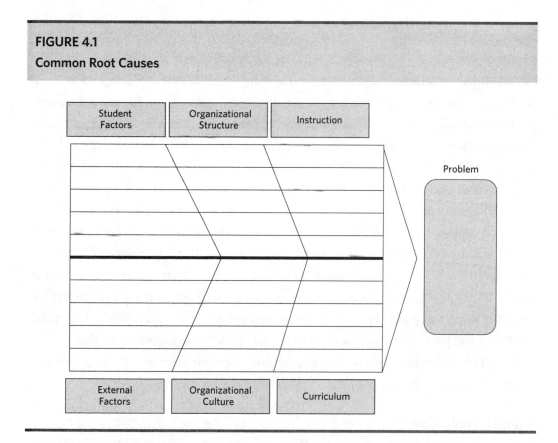

External Factors

Several factors external to the school contribute to the problems experienced by people within the school, including declining fiscal support, community crime rates, access to libraries and museums, and parent support. Like the student factors previously discussed, many of the external factors are beyond the control of the school yet are important to recognize. Understanding the realities does not mean that each must be addressed. Instead, the interventions will focus on root causes that people inside schools can control. For the staff of Mountain View, the external factor root causes were *gang recruitment in the local areas* and *limited parent involvement*. A teacher noted, "I know that there are deeper causes for why students might want to join a gang, so it may not really be a root cause, but I do like that we have it up there to remind us that there are things we could do to prevent students from wanting to join a gang."

Organizational Structure

School systems have a structure—the arrangement of responsibilities, authorities, and relationships among people—which is designed to facilitate effective and efficient work. For example, many schools have a principal, a counselor, a librarian, teachers, paraprofessionals, clerical staff, janitorial and grounds staff, and volunteers. An effective organizational structure ensures that each member of the organization understands her responsibilities and executes them well—toward a shared goal or aim. Sometimes the problem in an organization is that the individuals inside the organization are working toward different aims. In other cases, the organizational structure prevents work from being accomplished. At Mountain View, the organizational structure root causes were *limited accountability for what takes place in staff and department meetings* and *lack of collaboration time for content area teachers to meet and discuss their practices*. One teacher stated, "It's not like we ever get to meet up and talk as a department. I don't know if I'm doing the same things, or different things, as my peers." Another teacher commented, "We have great professional development but there isn't always accountability that we do anything to implement it. When we did the writing conventions, we were all accountable for implementing that. But that hasn't happened in math yet."

Organizational Culture

As we discussed in Chapter 3, schools have a culture that is noticeable and palpable. Sometimes the culture is positive and sometimes it's not. Culture is created and maintained by the people in the building. If neglected, the culture can become a contributing factor to the problems that need to be addressed. Root cause analysis focuses on solving a problem by looking at the causes, and it tends to shed light on the work that still needs to be done. Successes and celebrations do exist but aren't often discussed during root cause analysis work. For Mountain View, the organizational culture root cause was limited to the *types of interactions teachers have with each other,* which are uniformly positive. One of the teachers noted, "It's not in our culture to tell other people what to do or even to tell them when they can improve. I think that's getting in the way. We could be more honest, without hurting any feelings."

Instruction

As we have noted several times, instruction is key. What teachers do in their classrooms every day is really what matters most. Teachers have to seize every instructional moment and make it count. They have to engage, enlighten, and inspire their students through powerful instructional routines. Some aspects of instruction are more effective than others. Although we will not review these here, the evidence is clear that teachers should establish purpose, model their thinking, check for understanding and prompt or cue when errors are identified, structure group collaborative tasks, and hold students accountable for their learning. High-quality instruction cannot be left to chance; it must be planned and executed daily. For the teachers of Mountain View, the root causes related to instruction included *ineffective instructional strategies being used while teaching math, ineffective use of instructional minutes,* and *lack of test wiseness on behalf of students.* The latter is related to students being unfamiliar with test format, language, and layout. One of the teachers noted, "We're really good at some things in 6th grade, like teaching spelling. Well, really all of our language arts. That just doesn't seem to transfer very well to math. I'll personalize this one. I'm a way better teacher of language arts than I am of math. I think this is the root cause for me. I need to become better at teaching math, and knowing how to use the limited number of minutes we get for this subject."

Curriculum

What is taught is also important in terms of what students learn. Fourth graders taught 2nd grade content will go to 5th grade ready for 3rd grade content—and are still far behind. As part of the standards-based reform movement, the assessments are more directly linked with the standards, which means that teachers have to teach the expected standards if students are going to do well on the measures of those standards. Designing instruction that addresses grade level standards for students of that grade level will become increasingly important as 46 states (and counting) implement the Common Core State Standards and then assess students on one of the new tools. For the staff of

Mountain View, the curriculum root causes included *lack of alignment between the state assessment and the pacing guides* and *lack of permission to allocate additional instructional time on difficult content or content for which students did not reach mastery*. One teacher said, "It's not a surprise that the two areas our students score poorly on are measurement/geometry and the statistics/data analysis and probability. These are the two areas that have the least time devoted to them and stats come after the test. Maybe it's about revising the pacing guide and developing some formative assessments?"

Sphere of Influence or Sphere of Concern

For any complex education problem, many root causes will likely be at work. In some schools, the sheer number of root causes is overwhelming and causes paralysis in the system. In these cases, teams tend to dwell on the problems without being able to move forward to develop goals, objectives, and an intervention plan.

As part of the root causes analysis process, we have found it helpful to identify which of the causes are in our sphere of influence and which are in our sphere of concern. If this conversation doesn't happen, some members of the team may feel that the "real" issues are not being addressed. For example, at Liberty Elementary, the faculty wanted to address the identified problem of vocabulary. They identified several root causes, including:

- Nearly all students lived in poverty.
- Many students were English learners.
- A coherent vocabulary curriculum was missing.
- The professional development focus for the past several years was on fluency (which resulted in improved reading fluency scores).
- Students exhibited low levels of comprehension on grade-level reading tasks.
- Students had limited background knowledge.
- Limited classroom time was devoted to oral language or student-to-student interactions.

It could be argued that some of these issues are more likely contributing factors while others are more likely root causes, but the process the teachers at Liberty used was important in the development of their goals and interventions. After compiling their list of root causes, they drew two concentric circles on a large piece of paper to chart their responses. As they discussed each root cause, they were asked to identify if the factor was within the sphere of influence (the inner circle) or the sphere of concern (the outer circle). Their analysis can be found in Figure 4.2. This task allowed the team to decide which root causes it could influence, write goals and objectives for, and then target with interventions. It also allowed for all the issues, despite whether or not they could be addressed, to be named. As a kindergarten teacher noted, "I know that my students' vocabulary is limited due to their background knowledge and the fact that they live in

FIGURE 4.2
Comparing Sphere of Influence with Sphere of Concern

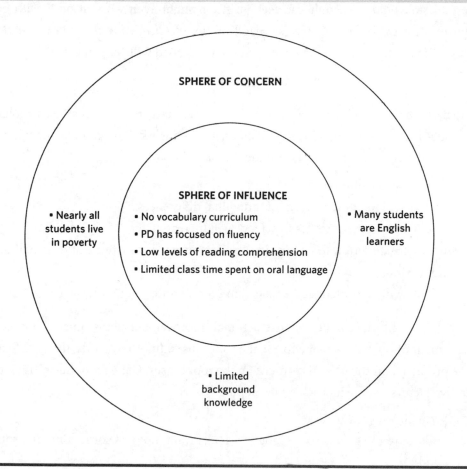

SPHERE OF CONCERN

SPHERE OF INFLUENCE

- No vocabulary curriculum
- PD has focused on fluency
- Low levels of reading comprehension
- Limited class time spent on oral language

- Nearly all students live in poverty

- Many students are English learners

- Limited background knowledge

poverty. I think it's important to recognize that and then move to things we can change. I want to create a vocabulary curriculum that will help, and make sure that we devote some instruction time to oral language."

Developing Goals and Objectives to Address the Root Causes

Once the problem or problems have been clarified and root causes have been explored, it's time to develop overarching goals and specific objectives. Setting goals and objectives is an important part of the instructional improvement process because they add accountability to the plan and can also be rallying points for a faculty. When people agree on a focus, their work will be directed toward that focus, and good things are more likely to happen. Without specific goals and objectives that are communicated clearly with a wide variety of stakeholders, people can feel adrift, or might even work at odds with other people in the organization. As Lewis Carroll, author of *Alice's Adventures in Wonderland*, suggests "If you don't know where you are going, any road will get you there."

Goals

Goals are broad statements of end results. They are targets to be hit as the problem is addressed. They tend to be motivational and help align work. For example, the following goals are from different schools in our local area:

- Literacy rates will improve.
- Students will be more tolerant of individual differences.
- Student achievement scores in science will increase.
- Student-to-student interactions in the classroom will constitute at least half of the instructional time.
- Students will be present and engaged in school more frequently.

The goals that are developed for instructional improvement plans must allow for the development of objectives that address the root causes. In other words, the goal focuses on the problem and the objectives focus on the root causes. Gene Donohue (2011) identified five factors to consider when developing goals:

1. Write down your goals.
2. Make sure the goal is something you really want, not just something that sounds good.

3. A goal cannot contradict any of your other goals.

4. Write your goal in the positive instead of the negative.

5. By all means, make sure your goal is high enough.

Although these factors were developed with self-improvement in mind, we have found them useful in guiding instructional improvement efforts. First, goals should be written so that they can be communicated widely and revisited regularly. The goals should be something that stakeholders really want, not something that is imposed on them or something that looks good to others.

Further, instructional improvement goals cannot contradict any of the other goals or processes. For example, if the school has a goal to increase student-to-student interaction in the classroom, it cannot have an observation tool that requires administrators to determine if the classroom is quiet and orderly. In terms of the way that goals are stated, people are more likely to work toward a positive goal rather than one suggesting that they should get rid of something. Rather than write "reduce absences," best practices suggest that the goal should include "increase attendance."

And perhaps most important, make sure that the goals that are developed are reasonable yet high enough to make a difference. An unreasonable goal will not rally stakeholders, nor will a goal that seems to be unworthy of time and attention. For example, in a school with 28 percent of the students proficient in English language arts, it might be unrealistic to have a one-year goal of 100 percent proficiency. That's not to say that high levels of proficiency are unattainable, but rather that huge jumps like this example are questioned, which can lead to apathy on the part of the people who need to work toward meeting the goal. In sum, good goals are realistic, obtainable, clearly stated, and used to align resources.

Objectives

Objectives are specific statements of student competency. As such, they should be

- Linked to specific behavior
- Clear and concise
- Observable
- Measurable
- Relevant to the instruction
- Microcosms of the related goal

Often, objectives are developed with the SMART criteria in mind: **S**pecific, **M**easurable, **A**ttainable, **R**elevant, and **T**imely.

SMART objectives can span a few weeks, such as "Within four weeks, all students in 4th grade will be able to convert the five primary fractions to decimals and percentages (halves, thirds, fourths, fifths, eighths, and tenths) with automaticity." Or SMART objectives can span an entire school year, such as "By the end of 3rd grade, all students will be able to write a three-paragraph essay using at least three types of introductions and three types of conclusions."

Returning to the discussion of Mountain View Middle School from Chapter 1, the stakeholders agreed to the following goals:

• Students at Mountain View Middle School will improve their state assessment math scores in statistics/probability and measurement/geometry.

• Students will improve their test wiseness skills for the math portion of the state assessment.

The specific objectives that they developed to meet these goals:

• Students will increase their scores on both the measurement/geometry and statistics strands of the state assessment from 42 percent to 65 percent proficient or advanced by the end of the school year.

• Students will score 80 percent or higher on the specified strands of common formative assessments to be given monthly.

• Students will score at least 8 out of 10 correct on weekly measurement/geometry and statistics quizzes that will include test-format questions as well as academic vocabulary.

Goals rally people within an organization to focus their work; objectives provide the benchmarks for determining success. In other words, objectives are important because they guide the development of an intervention plan and allow for monitoring the progress toward attainment of the goals. When an objective is clearly written, a plan for meeting that objective can be developed. As we will see in the next chapter, that intervention plan can involve direct work with students, professional development and coaching for teachers, curriculum revisions, or a host of other things. For example, the Mountain View Middle School intervention plan to meet the first objective involved redeveloping the professional development plans, providing peer coaching for teachers, and aligning units of study in a revised pacing guide. A clearly written objective also allows for the timely and regular review of hard and soft data to determine if progress has been made. For example, the Mountain View Middle School intervention plan to meet the second objective involved the development and use of common formative assessments that were administered, scored, and reviewed monthly.

Instructional Improvement in Action

The elementary school's data team, including Principal Mario Marcos, has reconvened to examine the hard and soft data collected over the past several weeks. In addition to the hard data provided by the state and the district, soft data had been collected in-house. These included individual interviews by the counselor with students suspended during the previous year, as well as survey data from teachers about curriculum alignment. These findings were compiled with other soft data, including the safe and secure schools survey results and the climate review commissioned the previous year. One member of the data team, a 3rd grade teacher who had been at the school for several years, served as the facilitator for the data walk. Using a process similar to the one described earlier in this chapter, the team members wrote questions and comments on their adhesive notes. In short order, they had sorted their notes and developed categories. As the newly appointed administrator, Mr. Marcos found this part of the process to be valuable because he was able to learn about the school's history of efforts for improvement. With the facilitator's help, the team developed these problem statements:

- There is a discrepancy in 3rd grade math scores, compared to 2nd and 4th grade. This cohort performed similarly low in 2nd grade. Given this two-year history, it is probable that the students will perform similarly low on this year's 4th grade test.
- The suspension and expulsion rate rose to its highest point in five years.
- Family participation in the school, as measured by volunteer hours and number of logged visits, declined by 27 percent last year.
- The attendance rate declined by 1 percent last year.

After developing the problem statements, the team turned its attention to a root cause analysis of each problem. The team reviewed each problem systematically, considering student and external factors, the organizational structure and climate, and curriculum and instruction. The team identified the following root causes for each problem.

- *Math scores:* Root causes include student factors such as higher numbers of English learners in this cohort, as well as curricular and instructional practices that do not emphasize supporting these learners in the development of academic language.
- *Suspension/expulsion:* The organization's current structure does not provide administrators with much flexibility in dealing with infractions. The organization's climate places a high value on punishment for misbehavior.
- *Family participation:* The organization's structure relies on the school's front office staff to address many problems. The staff members are frequently overwhelmed with dealing with too many problems simultaneously, especially immediately before and after school. In addition, the front office staff views triage, rather than hospitality, as its main mission during these times. Families do not feel welcome at the school.
- *Attendance:* Student factors and possible external factors appear to be the root causes of this decline. Twelve students from last year had absence and tardy rates that were significantly higher than the average attendance rate. Although the external factors are not yet understood, this situation warrants closer examination at the individual student level for each of these identified students.

Next, the team developed goals and objectives aligned to each problem and its root causes:

Goal 1: Fourth grade students will improve their math achievement.
- **Objective A:** Students will increase their scores on the math portion of the state assessment from 27 percent to 45 percent proficient or advanced by the end of the school year.
- **Objective B:** Students will score 80 percent or higher on common formative assessments to be given monthly.

Goal 2: The school will reduce suspension and expulsion rates.
- **Objective A:** Subgroup rates for suspension and expulsion will not exceed the school's demographic proportions in each quarter.
- **Objective B:** Each quarter's incidence of suspension and expulsion will be at least 40 percent lower than the last year's corresponding period.

Goal 3: Family participation rates will improve.
- **Objective A:** Family participation rates will improve by 10 percent in the first quarter compared with last year's corresponding period.

- **Objective B:** Cumulative family participation rates will improve by 30 percent at the midyear mark compared with last year's corresponding period.
- **Objective C:** Cumulative family participation will improve by 50 percent at the end of the year compared with last year.

Goal 4: Attendance rates of targeted students will improve.

- **Objective A:** Attendance rates of targeted students will be within 10 percent of the school mean attendance data at the end of the first marking period.
- **Objective B:** Attendance rates of targeted students will be within 7.5 percent of the school mean attendance data at the end of the first semester.
- **Objective C:** Attendance rates of targeted students will be within 5 percent of the school mean attendance data at the end of the school year.

The team members drew back to admire their work. They had accomplished much in the past few hours. "This is going to give us such good direction about the interventions we are going to need," said Mr. Marcos. "It sure is," noted the facilitator. "The discussion about the root causes is going to keep us focused. There's more work to do, but I can see a plan taking shape."

Quality Assurance

Like Warren Warwick, the physician introduced at the beginning of this chapter, the margin that separates good enough from great is the difference between 99.5 percent and 99.95 percent (Gawande, 2004). In education, the students who are tucked into this small space often represent those that are otherwise overlooked during conventional data analysis approaches. By purposefully foregrounding the academic and nonacademic experiences of students, staff, and community, we can unearth underlying problems that contribute to the more easily discoverable test score dilemmas. Test scores are important, of course. As organizations and professionals, this metric is continually used to evaluate us. But unless we examine the root causes of performance gaps, we cannot design targeted intervention. At best, we are left to try to treat the symptoms without ever addressing the illness.

Dr. Warwick's example offers another practice we are wise to adopt—monitoring the seemingly small changes that can add up to larger problems. By adopting a proactive approach, we begin to shift our gaze from looking backward to looking ahead. The interventions we design should thwart future problems, not just rectify past ones. As you examine your data for patterns and begin to craft problem statements, keep these quality assurance questions in mind:

- Are our visual displays of data aligned with the questions we have about our performance?
- Do our visual displays of data tell us a story? Is it an accurate story?
- Are we seeking patterns across data?
- Are we disciplined enough to focus on root causes first, and hold intervention in abeyance?
- Do we know the difference between our sphere of concern and our sphere of influence?
- Do our goals and objectives serve as signposts for where we need to go?

5

Mobilizing Efforts to Make a Difference

A well-known story about saving sea stars goes something like the following account.

> While walking along a beach, an elderly gentleman saw someone in the distance leaning down, picking something up, and throwing it into the ocean. As he got closer, he noticed that the figure was that of a young man, picking up sea stars one by one and tossing each gently back into the water. The old man smiled and said, "I must ask, then, why are you throwing sea stars into the ocean?"
>
> To this, the young man replied, "The sun is up and the tide is going out. If I don't throw them in, they'll die."
>
> Upon hearing this, the older man commented, "But, young man, do you not realize that there are miles and miles of beach and there are sea stars all along every mile? You can't possibly make a difference! You can't save them all."
>
> The young man listened politely. Then he bent down, picked up another sea star, threw it back into the ocean past the breaking waves and said, "I made a difference for that one."

And that's what many teachers and administrators all over the world do daily—save sea stars. We all know sea star savers and count ourselves lucky to have them at school. Personally, we have never been comfortable with that story and its message. It's always bothered us, but we really couldn't explain why. Perhaps it was the luck of the draw phenomenon that bothered us; whichever sea star was lucky enough to be close to the rescuer got attention. Or perhaps it was the idea that they couldn't all be saved or the suggestion that some were doomed by forces of nature. We really couldn't put our finger on it until we met Patrick.

When we met him, Patrick was in 9th grade and failing school. He had no credits to his name and was on probation for stealing. He lived in poverty, surrounded by drugs, gangs, and violence. He was one of many students who needed help, guidance, and support to be successful. But was he going to be a lucky sea star? His behavior wasn't great, so no one had focused on him. His attitude was terrible; in fact, he hated school. In other words, he wasn't likely to be selected by an adult for "saving."

Fortunately for Patrick, his cousin encouraged him to change schools to one where, as his cousin put it, "the teachers get in your business and really know you." In reality, Patrick's new school focused on instructional improvement as a never-ending quest. The school offered interventions at the individual level, group level, grade level, and whole school level. Patrick found himself part of several interventions, each designed to build his confidence and competence. Slowly, Patrick came to enjoy school and graduated college-ready. He made mistakes along the way and learned from each of them. When he wasn't kicked out for one of his transgressions, he said to a counselor, "This is the best school in the universe."

That's when we realized that Patrick taught us about sea stars. The message wasn't just about saving one and feeling good that you did. It was about creating structures so that they're all saved. Humans are not sea stars; we are not food for the next link in the chain. As such, we cannot accept that some students are left behind to fend for themselves. Instead, we have to create systems that address the goals and objectives we set. In other words, we have to mobilize the resources at our disposal around the plan that we have developed.

Selecting Interventions

Once your school has identified problems, determined the root causes, and developed goals and objectives, it's time to select interventions. This part of the process involves careful consideration of resources, both human and fiscal, as well as past experiences with success. The selected interventions should be possible to implement and some evidence should exist that they will result in positive changes so objectives can be met. Interventions can be selected in many ways. One consideration involves an understanding of the appropriate stakeholders. Should the intervention focus on students, faculty and staff, and/or families and community members? In addition, interventions can be directed to focus on different groups, from individuals to targeted groups, to grade level or content areas, or to the whole school. Many goals require interventions at various levels with various stakeholders. Figure 5.1 contains an example of various interventions as they fit into the matrix of type and group of stakeholders. In the sections that follow, we'll focus on

FIGURE 5.1
Sample Interventions

Focus of Intervention	Schoolwide	Grade Level or Content Area	Targeted Group	Targeted Individual
Students	• Restorative practices implemented schoolwide • Revised homework policy emphasizes spiral review	• Language development initiative in kindergarten • 12th grade students draft and revise college admissions essays	• Students who scored far below basic on state test attend mandatory tutorials • Students with disabilities participate in self-advocacy workshops • Boys who struggle both academically and with discipline participate in boys group	• Response to intervention for an identified student • Wraparound services and counseling for student with significant attendance issues • Use online intervention program to review and practice basic skills
Faculty and Staff	• Professional development on algebraic thinking skills • Daylong meeting to examine school data • Redesign of supervision duties to focus on playground safety	• Interdisciplinary units designed by 9th grade team • Professional learning community focusing on fostering argumentation • Grade-level effort on improving attendance	• Classroom management coaching and support for new teachers • Front office personnel attend professional development on creating a welcoming climate	• Coaching to improve instruction using gradual release of responsibility framework • Collegial coaching between teaching partners
Families and Community	• Use remind101.com (mass messaging) to provide sample test questions to family members • Schoolwide vaccination initiative to meet new enrollment guidelines	• Financial aid training for 11th grade families • Parent-Teacher Literacy and Math Nights for incoming 6th grade families	• Career-development community mentors assigned for gifted and talented students • Language education classes offered for interested families during school day	• Counseling about child's attendance • Provide parent access to BookShare so that reading materials are available at home

each stakeholder group and explore in greater detail the types of interventions that can be used to meet objectives. We provide several illustrative examples of the range of interventions that schools can use. Although this list is not exhaustive, it is a collection of ideas that can be used as fodder for the types of interventions needed to address the problems, root causes, and goals and objectives that are developed at each school.

Students

Nearly every school improvement effort begins with the work of directly affecting the academic, social, and behavioral skills of its students (Muijs, Harris, Chapman, Stoll, & Russ, 2004). Although these efforts are often accomplished through a multilevel approach that includes faculty and staff as well as families and communities, virtually no plan would overlook the ways in which a school can affect student achievement. But in the rush to develop interventions for specific students or groups of students, one essential element can be forgotten—high-quality core instruction. Because instruction and intervention are inexorably linked, a reform effort that ignores one while focusing on the other weakens both (California Department of Education, 2008). Using the familiar language of Response to Intervention (RTI), Tier 1 is defined as quality core instruction. A school that does not have 75 percent of its students near grade level is wise to turn its attention to improving this area first. (Tier 2 supplemental interventions and Tier 3 intensive individualized interventions will be discussed later in this section.) See Figure 5.2 for a visual of the RTI model.

High-quality core instruction relies on a gradual release of responsibility model, first articulated by Pearson and Gallagher (1983). We have further expanded the original model as an instructional framework, which includes the following elements:

• *Focus lessons* that are brief in nature, usually 5 to 15 minutes in length. These lessons include establishing the purpose for the day's lesson and contain the content, language, and if developmentally appropriate, the social purpose (Fisher & Frey, 2011). In addition, the teacher models or demonstrates and thinks aloud about his cognitive and metacognitive thinking.

• *Guided instruction*, which occurs as the teacher releases cognitive responsibility to students to give them an opportunity to apply newly learned concepts and skills. The teacher is present to scaffold their understanding, using robust questions, prompts, and cues (Fisher & Frey, 2010b).

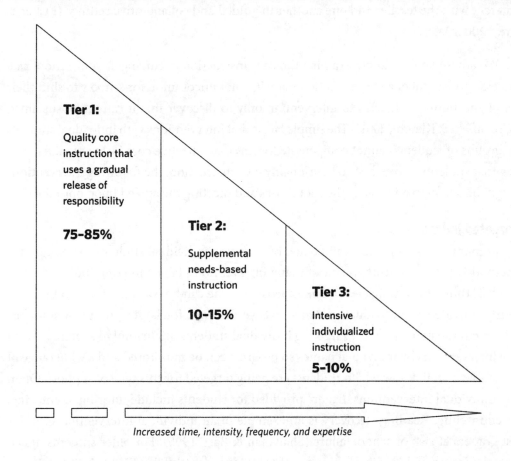

FIGURE 5.2
Tiers of Intervention

Tier 1:

Quality core instruction that uses a gradual release of responsibility

75–85%

Tier 2:

Supplemental needs-based instruction

10–15%

Tier 3:

Intensive individualized instruction

5–10%

Increased time, intensity, frequency, and expertise

Source: Fisher, D., & Frey, N. (2010). *Enhancing RTI: How to ensure success with effective classroom instruction and intervention.* Alexandria, VA: ASCD. Used with permission.

- *Collaborative learning* in the form of productive group work (Frey, Fisher, & Everlove, 2009). In this phase of instruction, students work in the company of peers to resolve problems using the academic language of the lesson. This phase is crucial for students as it promotes interaction, develops language, and reinforces the content and social skills needed for learning.

- *Independent learning*, which includes both in- and out-of-class learning, such as homework. Regardless of the venue, the independent phase of learning should occur only after students are approaching mastery and have had multiple opportunities to interact with the teacher and one another in guided and collaborative settings (Fisher & Frey, 2008b).

We advise you to closely examine the core instruction occurring at your school as a necessary element of any intervention plan. It is not uncommon for schools to shift their fiscal and human resources to intervention only to discover that it cannot be sustained (Greenfield & Klemm, 2001). The simple fact is that interventions with individual students or groups of students cannot compensate for less than effective core instruction. Assuming that students have access to high-quality core instruction, the following interventions might be useful in addressing the root causes and meeting the agreed upon objectives.

Targeted Individual

In many cases, objectives can be met by targeting individual students. Although this method is a valuable component of many intervention plans, targeting individual students is time-consuming and can be expensive. Time can be wasted if interventions are being provided to individual students that would work for larger groups of students. When circumstances require targeting individual students, it's helpful to keep records of the interventions by individual names so progress can be monitored and a wide range of stakeholders will know which students are being targeted for this type of support. Often the individual interventions that are provided for students include tutoring, mentoring, or counseling. Reading Recovery is an example of an individual intervention used for 1st graders at risk of school failure (Shanahan & Barr, 1995). For older students, it can be useful to provide individual lessons that build students' skills. Figure 5.3 contains an example of a lesson plan format for individualized instruction in literacy. In addition, intervention programs are available online that provide for practice and reinforcement of skills. As a cautionary note, although useful, these programs cannot replace the need for skilled teachers to provide instruction and intervention for students (Fisher & Ivey, 2006). What they can do is provide additional time on task for students to practice the skills they have been taught.

One of the objectives that the team at Franklin Elementary School identified focused on English proficiency for English learners. The school had several students who were not making progress but rather were performing at intermediate levels of proficiency for

FIGURE 5.3

Individualized Lesson Plan Format

Student _____   Teacher _____

Date _____

| Familiar Book: Level: |
| Result of Observation: |

| New Book: Level: |
| Targeted skills for this lesson: |
| Standards: |

| Book Introduction: |

| Word Work: Writing: |

| Student Reading: |

| Questions: |

several years in a row. The team identified several root causes, one of which was the fact that no English learners were ever referred for special education assessments. One of the teachers noted, "I think that there are some students learning English who do have learning disabilities. It's probably not a lot, but maybe 10 percent or so, like students who are native speakers. We have no English learners at our school who get special education services. That's just as bad as over-representation." To address this problem and meet the objective, the team agreed to implement intensive intervention as part of their RTI efforts for students who had performed at intermediate proficiency for three or more years (Fisher, Frey, & Rothenberg, 2011). Each of the students would receive individual instruction in academic language, and weekly performance data would be collected to determine if progress was made. Consistent with RTI efforts, if a specific student did not make progress, she would be referred for more formal special education assessments to determine eligibility.

Targeted Group

Some interventions can be delivered to groups of students, especially when the group has similar needs. Targeting a specific group of students can maximize the limited resources most schools devote to intervention. Several different interventions can be used with targeted students. For example, small group instruction, with no more than six members, has been effective in meeting the needs of some students (Vaughn, Hughes, Moody, & Elbaum, 2001). This type of instruction is consistent with Tier 2 interventions in RTI in which students receive supplemental interventions based on their assessed needs on a regular basis. Typically these types of interventions occur several times per week for 20 to 30 minutes each day. In other cases, a targeted group of students may meet after school or during a designated part of the school day. For example, students who are frequently absent may meet with the school social worker as a targeted group to discuss their need to remain in school, attend classes, focus on schoolwork, and develop habits for becoming lifelong learners. Given their shared experience and need, namely not attending school, when they meet as a group they can discuss the challenges in their lives while the social worker is available to mediate and provide support.

The targeted group does not need to have a remedial focus. One of the unintended effects of the No Child Left Behind Act has been the inattention to students who are gifted and talented (DeLacy, 2004). At Mar Vista Elementary School, teachers wanted to address the problem of the declining percentage of students who score at the advanced level on the state assessment. A group of students who had performed at much higher levels in previous years was now performing at a lower proficient level. These students were still scoring at grade level, but this dip, seemingly minor at first glance, was noticed by the data team as it examined hard data for trends. The team examined root causes and determined through individual interviews that these students could easily do the assigned work and generally enjoyed school, but were not really challenged with complex tasks. The team formed an intervention group with 24 of these students and created a schedule so the group could meet with the vice principal three times per week. As part of the intervention, the target group was challenged with increasingly complex tasks that were used to replace those assigned in the students' respective classrooms. The students also were tasked with serving as peer tutors in their classrooms and received instruction in how to guide peers to understanding rather than telling them the answers.

At Rady High School, the team wanted to address the problem of a small group of juniors who had not passed the high school exit exam. The team's goal was for all students to pass the exit exam by the end of 11th grade. The team identified the strand of writing strategies as the barrier for most students who had not passed the high-stakes test. They discussed root causes and believed that these students did not have enough instruction in writing strategies as tested. In discussing the root causes, one teacher said, "These are all great kids. I'm kind of surprised by the names on the list. I think that they just don't know how to edit like the test expects, because their writing scores are very good overall." The team decided to implement an after-school intervention two days per week, focused on writing strategies that would be taught by several of the English teachers. One of the teachers said, "We're going to have some selling to do to make sure that they don't see this as punishment. We have to make it fun and have some sort of celebrations of successes along the way."

Grade Level or Content Area

Moving to a larger scale, some interventions are more appropriate to conduct at grade level or in the content area. A larger scale intervention is especially useful when evidence shows that the majority of students at that grade or in that content area need additional instruction. This intervention also requires some attention to the teachers of the grade or content, which will be discussed later. Numerous interventions can be implemented at grade or in the content area to help students. For example, Success for All (Borman, Slavin, Cheung, Chamberlain, Madden, & Chambers, 2007) provides grade-level regrouping to ensure that all students receive supplemental instruction and intervention. The Success for All approach requires that all students in a given grade participate in the intervention, and evidence supports it as a success. Other interventions focus on specific content areas, such as developing an inquiry approach to science (Minner, Levy, & Century, 2010), integrating technology into learning (McCormack & Ross, 2010), teaching historical thinking skills and using primary and secondary sources in social studies (Reisman, 2012), or implementing cognitively guided instruction in mathematics (Carpenter, Fennema, & Franke, 1996). Each intervention changes the educational experience for a larger group of students, but also has implications for the work of teachers because interventions selected in one area will have corresponding implications for other areas.

In addition to the focus on proficiency for English learners discussed earlier, the faculty at Franklin Elementary School also selected an intervention focused on grade-level support. Third grade appeared to be the sticking point for many students. More than 90 percent of the students were making progress between kindergarten and 2nd grade, but those percentages started dropping in 3rd grade and continued to drop each subsequent year. As part of an effort to address the root cause and meet the objective, the team members decided to target 3rd grade for additional English language development instruction. They decided to purchase a supplemental curriculum that could be used to help students reach a new level of achievement. Like many interventions at grade level or in the content area, this change created implications for teacher professional development. In its meeting, the team discussed the implications for the new supplemental curriculum, and one teacher stated, "We really have to do something now if we are going to meet this objective. We can't take on the whole problem, but we could start with 3rd grade. I know that this means that all of the 3rd grade teachers will have to alter their schedules, but I'm willing to do that, and help the others, because I believe that this is the right intervention for my students."

Schoolwide

Sometimes interventions can be developed and implemented that affect the entire school. Growing evidence shows that schoolwide interventions should be considered in any instructional improvement effort (Allington & Gabriel, 2012). Those interventions often require that students experience some consistency throughout the day. In some schools, school is unpredictable for students and they spend a great deal of time focused on how they are being taught rather than what they are supposed to learn. For example, a failing high school selected four schoolwide interventions that the staff and faculty believed would positively affect student achievement: wide reading, shared reading, note-taking, and writing to learn (Fisher, Frey, & Lapp, 2009). Other schoolwide efforts improve attendance and tardiness (Tyre, Feuerborn, & Pierce, 2011) and reduce bullying (McNamee & Mercurio, 2008). What interventions at the schoolwide level have in common is that all students experience the intervention.

The teachers at Johnson Elementary School decided that they needed a schoolwide intervention to meet their objective focused on improving mathematics achievement. Their root cause analysis suggested that students at Johnson experience math content as bits and parts. One teacher said, "Our students know how to do some math, but they don't see how it connects with their thinking. They solve some problems and can crank out some answers, but their thinking isn't there yet." As a result, the team members decided that they would focus on algebraic thinking at all grades, K–6, so the students would experience a more cohesive, thinking-based mathematics curriculum rather than a curriculum focused on procedures. As with other schoolwide interventions, making this decision meant that the teachers would have to reconsider their curriculum and instruction and would likely need additional professional development along with dedicated time in their professional learning communities. However, the team members decided to leave the intervention listed at the student level because they wanted to focus on the experience that students would have, understanding that there would be associated implications for teachers, staff, parents, and administrators.

Faculty and Staff

Without question, investment in the expertise of the teaching staff is a wise move. In their seminal longitudinal study on the efforts of a high school undergoing reform, Darling-Hammond, Ancess, and Ort (2002) cited several factors that relate to the school's success:

- A purposeful and coherent curriculum
- Explicit teaching of academic skills
- Multiple strategies for active learning
- Performance assessment
- Collaborative planning and professional development

Student successes were achieved not only by affecting the direct student experiences, such as restructuring for before- and after-school supports, but also investing in teachers. Every school has excellent teachers; some schools have many. But without a cohesive plan for ensuring that their effective approaches spread, excellence remains within silos, and students are not able to capitalize on the magnified multiyear effects of access to a series of fine teachers (e.g., Chetty, Friedman, & Rockoff, 2011; Sanders, 2000). The evidence on the effectiveness of professional development is strong, but must include certain conditions, including differentiation, opportunities for follow-up, and coaching (e.g., Joyce & Showers, 2002; Van Driel & Berry, 2012).

Although there is limited research on the role of professional development for non-instructional staff, studies on school climate speak to the importance of their efforts in building a collegial atmosphere. A longitudinal study of a two-year school climate reform initiative found that the organizational structures outside of the classroom had a profound effect on student, teacher, and family perceptions of the school (Tschannen-Moran & Tschannen-Moran, 2011). This relationship between organizational structures and perceptions was attributed to the coordinated efforts of instructional and noninstructional staff around three reoccurring themes: student achievement and success, trust and respect, and community pride and involvement. Schools that invest in coordinated efforts between faculty and staff regarding climate and culture ensure that these positive behaviors are modeled each day, by every adult on campus (Fisher, Frey, & Pumpian, 2012). And, as with students, there are times when interventions are needed to address gaps in achievement and performance.

Targeted Individual

At times, specific people on the staff need attention. Classified staff members may need support understanding and executing their jobs. For example, Centennial High School's new custodian believed that he would be fired if he interacted with students. As part of an objective to make the campus friendlier, the staff at Centennial targeted this specific employee. During a discussion with a vice principal, the custodian shared that he had been told by peers from other schools that he should stay away from the students because "they can blame you for things you didn't do." In this case, the conversation helped this staff member understand his role, allowed him to ask questions about boundaries and limits, and provided the administrator an opportunity to clarify the vision of the school with an employee who did not yet understand it.

Although targeting an individual staff member can be awkward and potentially embarrassing for the person, it does not have to be. For example, a wide range of coaching options can be used to help teachers improve their practice. Having a peer coach does not necessarily mean that a teacher is ineffective. We all have been recipients of coaching at various points in our careers, and we are better for it. Individual support for teachers through coaching should be part of a larger professional development initiative. As noted by Darling-Hammond and McLaughlin (1995), the essential characteristics of teacher professional development include the following:

- It must engage teachers in concrete tasks of teaching, assessment, observation, and reflection that illuminate the processes of learning and development.
- It must be grounded in inquiry, reflection, and experimentation that are participant-driven.
- It must be collaborative, involving a sharing of knowledge among educators and a focus on teachers' communities of practice rather than on individual teachers.
- It must be connected to and derived from teachers' work with their students.
- It must be sustained, ongoing, intensive, and supported by modeling, coaching, and the collective solving of specific problems of practice.
- It must be connected to other aspects of school change. (p. 597)

Although the list extends beyond the individual teacher, it is important to note the connection between sustained professional development and coaching for individual teachers who need assistance solving problems of practice.

As one of their objectives, the faculty and staff at Museum Charter School focused on problem-based learning because one of the root causes they unearthed suggested that students found some of their classes boring and thus did not want to focus on the work. Students viewed the problem-based learning they did in other classes as engaging. As one of the interventions, the team decided to survey students about classes and situations that were relevant and interesting and those that were not. The faculty members agreed that they would address the survey results honestly and work to support one another in improving students' experiences. Teachers were also encouraged to ask for help from their peers if they felt that they were not fully implementing problem-based learning. Mr. Artiaga, a 4th grade teacher, volunteered, saying, "I'm new here, well, starting last year. I suspect that my classes will be rated a little lower than some of the others. I don't really understand how to structure all of the tasks required in problem-based learning, but I'm open to learning how." Ms. Jeffers, a 2nd grade teacher, volunteered to serve as his coach, noting, "That's the spirit I like; we can always improve. I'd love to show you what I'm doing, so long as you'll give me some feedback about it. I'm always looking to learn."

Targeted Group

As with students, groups of staff members may have similar needs resulting from their experience or beliefs. Regardless of the source, grouping similar staff members can allow schools to address root causes and meet the established objectives while maximizing resources. For example, when they decided to make the school a more welcoming place, the team members at Centennial High School also noted that they should intervene with the front office staff. One of the parents on the team noted, "It's not like they're rude or anything. In fact, they're really very nice. It's just that they seem so busy and we hate to bother them. But when you really need something, you have to bother them, and then you feel bad." As part of the intervention plan, the administration was tasked with organizing a workflow analysis. The group members identified specific responsibilities that had to be completed at specific times and provided space away from public view for staff to complete some of these tasks. They also met with the staff members more often to communicate the valued role they held in the school and to respond to questions or issues that arose that took the staffers away from their primary tasks.

Sometimes the target groups are easy to identify, as is the case with teachers new to the profession. Although some schools and districts offer induction support, if the school is focused on instructional improvement, the generic induction support program may not be sufficient to address the root causes and meet the outlined objectives. At Taft Elementary, the district offered a strong induction support system for teachers, mainly focused on classroom management and organization. But Taft was a school in trouble, and the team members understood that they could not wait a few years to focus their intervention efforts. One of the interventions was designed to improve reading comprehension scores, so the team targeted new teachers and provided them with release days to observe veteran teachers, group meetings to examine curriculum, and opportunities to ask questions and discuss challenges with senior staff members.

Although some individuals may fit into a group based on their needs to radically improve their instructional repertoires, this situation is not within the purview of the entire faculty or the data review team. These situations are best left to the administrator and the evaluation process. Having said that, the administrator can deploy some of the interventions listed in this chapter as part of the plan to help these teachers improve their practices.

Grade Level or Content Area

As we discussed in the section on grade-level and content-area interventions for students, sometimes the intervention requires that teachers come together to address a problem. Often, this intervention occurs as part of a professional learning community (PLC) (DuFour, DuFour, Eaker, & Karhanek, 2004) in which a grade-level or content-area group of teachers meets to examine practices. Of course, PLCs can also involve targeted groups of teachers or be self-selected. But for the intervention plan, the formation of the group will likely be at the grade level or in the content area. Typically, PLC members discuss four questions during their time together:

1. What do we want all students to know and be able to do?
2. How will we know what students have learned?
3. What will we do when they don't know or learn it?
4. What will we do when they do know or learn it?

As part of an intervention plan, the PLC work can be directed toward a specific problem or a specific group of students. For example, at Franklin Elementary School, the PLC groups were charged with focusing on long-term English learners. In every meeting, the PLCs responded to the four main questions focused on English learners. Those sessions were in addition to the other interventions they identified to address this problem. At Johnson Elementary School, the PLC meetings were focused on algebraic thinking as part of the overall plan to improve students' understanding of the thinking behind the mathematics they were learning.

In addition to PLCs, the grade-level or content-area intervention may need to focus on curricular changes. Sometimes a mismatch occurs between what is actually being taught and what was supposed to be taught, which was the case at Watson High School as the teachers attempted to address the low levels of achievement in world history. The students were scoring well in other classes within the same grade level. As a group, the teachers examined root causes and noted that the world history curriculum was not well aligned. In fact, the teachers realized that the curriculum for the first six weeks was a review of content covered in previous years and was not, in fact, in the standards for their grade level. The intervention required that the world history teachers revise their curriculum and develop new pacing guides that were better aligned with the content that was expected to be taught.

Schoolwide

Reeves (2004) has noted that schools can beat the odds when they have a focus. In fact, having a schoolwide focus is one of the conditions for school success, but reaching agreement isn't easy. Many demands compete for attention, and the individuals within schools have different ideas about what's important. When the faculty and staff do reach consensus on a focus and then align their work toward that focus, impressive changes and outcomes can occur. One of the best ways to develop a schoolwide focus is to carefully examine data and identify root causes. Then faculty and staff are more likely to put their differences aside and agree to focus on an issue that they believe will help their students, especially when they realize that their colleagues are willing to do the same.

At Dr. Martin Luther King Jr. Elementary School, the team was focused on reading comprehension. The scores in this area were far below the scores on the other subtests in language arts. To the team's surprise, students even did better on vocabulary subtests than they did on reading comprehension. In their analysis of root causes, the team members realized that informational texts were hard to find within the school, and even when they were present, they were rarely taught. Instead, the texts were left for independent reading. Given the widespread nature of the problem, they wanted to develop a schoolwide intervention but knew they would need a lot more support from colleagues. At the next scheduled faculty meeting, the team raised the issue of informational texts. Toward the end of the discussion, one teacher said, "You know, I'm going to do this. I'm going to teach more informational texts. I really do like stories better, but I see that my students need to know how to read this kind of text and I'm not doing a very good job of teaching them to do so." By the end of the meeting, the faculty and staff committed to teaching with informational texts at least 50 percent of the time. They also knew that they would have to appeal to the community for support in obtaining more informational texts and agreed to add that as an intervention as well.

At Harborside High School, the faculty and staff wanted to address their identified problem, which was the historically low number of students who went on to college. During their root cause analysis, they came to understand that the vast majority of students were college-eligible but didn't actually attend. When the team looked to the root cause for students not attending, it was discovered that students were generally afraid of college, didn't know what it would be like, and didn't know if they could afford it. As part of a schoolwide intervention, the faculty agreed to organize several college visits, invite current college students to make short presentations and answer questions in classes, and to hire a paraprofessional who understood college admissions and financial aid to mentor students. Students at every grade—not just seniors—were involved with this intervention, and students in every grade visited college campuses. The faculty created a visitation schedule by grade, which also included guest speakers from those colleges to visit high school classes.

Families and Community

Schools don't exist in isolation; they are contextualized by their relationships within families and the larger community. In fact, the level of support schools receive, both fiscal and human, is directly related to the regard in which they are held by these stakeholders. Warren (2011) argues that schools should actively cultivate these relationships in part to create far-reaching advocacy networks. Writing from the lens of urban schools, the author states that "strong and sustained progress in school reform may require moving beyond 'the four walls of schools' to engage the participation of parents and residents" of the community (p. 485). Similarly, Boykin and Noguera (2011) note that parents and community members from low-income and urban schools have been left out of school improvement efforts.

Increasing family involvement in a child's education has had noteworthy successes at all levels. These documented effects include literacy gains among preschoolers (Hindman & Morrison, 2011), improved academic achievement in high school science (Shumow, Lyutykh, & Schmidt, 2011), and improved high school graduation rates of Hispanic adolescents (Chun & Dickson, 2011). These and other studies suggest that parent involvement should not be measured simply by the number of volunteer hours at the school or even the number of times a family visits the school, especially in middle and high school. These direct participation measures decrease over time as children grow, and measures need to include more than just foot traffic. Measures of soft data such as interviews, focus groups, and surveys—about feeling a sense of belonging, perceptions of school climate, and parent efficacy in their child's education—can assist a school in tracking progress and developing appropriate interventions.

Targeted Individual

As with students and staff members, at times the appropriate intervention is focused on an individual parent or community member. This intervention may be due to significant absence on the part of a student or because a community member has resources that the school can use. For example, at Del Sol Middle School, three students had attendance rates lower than 40 percent, meaning that they missed more than 60 percent of the school year. As part of their intervention efforts, the faculty members of Del Sol decided to target the family members of these students. They discovered that one student had become the primary caregiver for her grandmother, who had diabetes and chronic obstructive pulmonary disease. Another student was experiencing early onset mental health challenges, and the family was trying to deal with the situation without outside help, and without much luck. The third student missed school due to conflicts at home. He frequently was in trouble with the law and often ran away for days on end. The parents did not know what to do next and welcomed the efforts of the school. Each of these situations is so different from the others, which is why individual interventions are important. Although it would be difficult to provide this level of intensity to every student in the school, targeting some students is possible and will likely allow the school to meet instructional improvement goals and objectives.

Beyond school and family, some individuals and agencies in the community can be included in school improvement intervention plans. For example, the team at Harborside High School focused on a local foundation that had previously provided funds for students to participate in field studies as part of their science curriculum. The team members decided to focus on this foundation again as part of their intervention efforts to ensure that the support they received in the past would continue, especially given that the previous efforts had resulted in improved achievement.

Targeted Group

As with the other stakeholders, when needs cluster into groups, a target group is appropriate for intervention. In the case of families and community members, there are times when bringing a group together is effective. For example, to ensure that all students passed the high school exit exam by 11th grade, the team at Rady High School decided to intervene with the family members and make home visits for each student who had yet to pass the exam. The team also provided this target group with supplemental materials that the students could use as practice for the content that would be assessed. One of the teachers noted, "We should meet with the target parents every few weeks as well. If we just meet with them once, the practice work could be overwhelming. I think it's better to give them the practice work after we've covered it with the students so we know that the students know how to do it."

At Taft Elementary, faculty and staff targeted a group of alumni from the school, especially retirees, who could return for a few hours per week to read with students, tutor them, and be a source of support for the school. In their e-mail messages, phone calls, and letters requesting volunteers, they noted the pride that alumni felt and how important it was to give back to the school. The team provided volunteers with a dedicated room to store their belongings, a coffee cup with their name and the school's name, and short lessons on how to tutor students.

Grade Level or Content Area

When a grade level or content area is targeted, the team must consider how the intervention efforts will be communicated with family members. If familiar routines and contacts change, families want to know about it. Most important, if interventions are made in response to a need, families can work in concert with the school to realize the necessary changes. Intervening with family and community members can be handled in different ways, and they all include open invitations for everyone involved in the life of a student at that grade or in the class. For example, family literacy or family math nights are an effort to help parents help their children. These "all call" events are typically focused on a specific content area and a specific grade. They can be effective in creating homes that are more school-like, as well as schools that are more home-like (Frey, 2010).

As part of the intervention efforts at Mar Vista Elementary School, the team decided to focus on homework, specifically for students who had previously performed at the advanced proficiency level but who were no longer performing that well on state assessments. The school had previously changed its homework policies to be spiral review, meaning that the work sent home was familiar to students and provided students an opportunity to practice and apply things that they had been taught. However, during their root cause analysis work, the staff at Mar Vista learned that parents were doing a lot of homework for their children. When asked about doing the homework, most of the parents said that they wanted their children to be seen as "good and smart" by the teachers. The parents did not seem to understand that the result was that students were doing less work and performing less well. So the team held grade-level homework clinics with parents to teach them how to assist their children without doing the work for them. Interestingly, the attendees at these clinics were not limited to parents. There were grandparents, older siblings, aunts and uncles, and even neighbors who came to learn more about how to help.

Schoolwide

Some interventions target all family members or a wide range of community members. Often, these are communication-related interventions, which tend to involve getting the word out to the community. For example, middle and high schools across California were required to verify a new immunization or deny a student admission or attendance. The requirement was a statewide focus, but some schools wrote an intervention into their plan, especially schools that had attendance-related goals and objectives. At Harborside, the team developed a communication system to send daily notifications to parents who had not yet produced immunization verification. The intervention team also met with students who still needed verification and scheduled the department of health to provide the immunization on campus during the first week of school to help meet the deadline a month later.

Similarly, when bullying was targeted by the staff members of Avondale Elementary School, they created a public awareness campaign that included information for parents and community members. In their root cause analysis, they learned that some families did not believe bullying was happening and other families encouraged students to "show how tough they were," which was being misinterpreted by some students as permission to bully others. The intervention campaign included information about the harm that bullies inflict on others as well as the consequences for the bully. The staff members created flyers, mailers, and an Internet web page, all targeted at family and community members. Their plan also had other interventions, including targeting the bullies as well as the bystanders, but a major part of their efforts focused on educating families and community members.

Instructional Improvement in Action

The data team at Mario Marcos's elementary school reviewed the hard and soft data to identify problems and had engaged in extensive discussion about root causes. In addition, the team developed goals and objectives aligned to each of these problems, but developing interventions would need to involve the entire staff. The following week, the principal and the data team presented data in a meeting for all the adults in the school, hosting similar data walks so participants could understand the data. The team then presented findings and problem statements, and shared goals and objectives for each one. At each juncture, the findings were discussed and in some cases revised. For instance, several staff members discussed the importance of using more nuanced measures of family involvement beyond the number of visits and volunteer hours.

After refining the goals and objectives, the work of identifying interventions began. These interventions were not determined in a single meeting; a committee was formed for each of the four identified problems, and the adults on the campus participated in one of them. Over the next several weeks, the committees looked more closely at their assigned topic, including examining the research around effective interventions and methods of measurement for formative assessments. In a faculty–staff meeting, spokespersons for each committee proposed an intervention plan. The 4th grade math committee suggested providing professional development for teachers on strategies for fostering academic language for English learners, assessing each student in the first week of school in mathematics to identify students in need of intervention, and developing and administering monthly formative assessments aligned to the state exam.

The second committee was charged with reducing the school's suspension and expulsion rates. This group proposed professional development in restorative practices, sponsored by the International Institute of Restorative Practices, for the entire school. The members noted that this work would be a multiyear effort and suggested creating a working group to analyze the logistics and outcomes of these efforts. "There are a lot of dimensions to taking on this kind of work, including student education, family involvement, and building our own internal expertise," one member said. "We think that this work group should serve in an advisory capacity for the administration," she continued. "Over time, I can really see this including student and family representatives."

Next, the third committee reported on its work surrounding family participation. Taking a lead from the discussion that had occurred at the previous data meeting, this group recommended looking at parent perceptions as well as number of visits. The group proposed increasing the number of school newsletters for families, suggesting that grade levels work together to produce one per week. In addition, the committee advised that these newsletters should be made available electronically and on paper, and suggested that the school obtain a text notification system and an auto-dialer to reach families. "This would strengthen our emergency notification system, of course, but we could be using it much more frequently to send greetings, reminders, and other content messages," offered the committee's spokesperson. "Our initial goal is to up the number of contacts we make with families during the course of the year." The committee also proposed that each teacher make contact with at least two families per week via e-mail message or phone call to relay a positive message about their child. "We'd like for families to really see how much we care about their children. We know we do, but we don't always take the time to tell families," he said. As a final proposal, the committee suggested charging the school's parent–teacher organization with developing and administering a survey to elicit suggestions from families about improvement.

The final committee rose to speak about attendance. As noted by the data team, there were 12 students the previous year who accounted for a disproportionate number of absences. "Ten of these students are slated to be here this year," said one committee member. "We'd like to target these children and their families immediately to support their improved attendance. This is going to involve individual meetings with families and students, and we know that this will put an increased burden on the administrative team, but we think it's really important." To be more proactive, the committee recommended doing a sweep of absences each month to identify any other students exceeding a 10 percent rate. "There's a lot of evidence that students who are absent for 10 percent or more of the school year do poorly, and we anticipate that there are going to be other services, like counseling, the school nurse, or the social worker that will need to be involved," said the spokesperson.

After the committees presented their proposals, Mr. Marcos told the faculty and staff that there would be a one-week commenting period for everyone to digest the information, ask questions, and refine interventions. "No one should leave this meeting thinking that everything is set in stone, or that we only have to talk about interventions once a year. We'll have to finalize our plan and figure out how we're going to monitor it. In the meantime," the principal offered, "I want to thank all of you for your work and collaboration. I can't imagine how our students wouldn't be successful, when they are surrounded by such caring adults."

Quality Assurance

The development of a sound intervention plan must begin with high-quality core instruction. No matter how robust the intervention is, it simply cannot replace instructional excellence for every student, every day. Having said that, interventions at the individual level, for a targeted group, across a grade level or in a content area, and even schoolwide make sense. These levels of intervention should also look across stakeholders and include students, faculty and staff, and families and community members. By singling out only one group, we limit the scope and therefore the likely effectiveness of any intervention. The school is really a nested system of relationships, and interventions should be similarly designed.

As you design and refine your intervention plan, consider these quality assurance questions:

- Have we assessed the core instruction that all students receive? Do we need to make changes in the core instruction?

- Do the interventions correspond to the identified root causes? Is each root cause addressed?

- Does the intervention plan include all stakeholders—students, faculty and staff, families, and the community?

- Does the intervention plan address varying levels of involvement—targeted individuals, targeted groups, grade levels or content areas, and the entire school?

- Are there implications from an intervention in one area that are not addressed in another area, such as a student intervention that will require teacher professional development?

6

Monitoring Progress and Midcourse Corrections

A product on the market is designed to monitor sleep cycles, silently waking up the wearer at the ideal time, and to monitor—and thus encourage—physical activity. The makers of this product suggest that monitoring leads to a healthier lifestyle. Large-scale studies support the advertising claim that simply tracking activity leads to a 26 percent increase in activity levels. For example, Bravata and colleagues (2007) found that people who monitored their physical activity with a pedometer averaged 2,700 more steps per day than those who did not. The activity, in turn, led to a significant decrease in body mass index and blood pressure. In other words, they were healthier. Those who choose to monitor activity level really do engage in activity more frequently. We have tried the device and agree that these claims are accurate. Knowing that you haven't taken your 10,000 steps—directly facing the data—can spur you to action. For example, the reading on Nancy's pedometer encouraged her to set aside her laptop and go for a walk on her treadmill—and Diane wears the device on her pajamas to make sure that she gets credit for her last steps of the evening.

A pedometer is just one of many tools that we all use to monitor events in our lives. We have smoke detectors to monitor the air quality. We use thermostats to monitor the temperature in our houses, and we adjust the setting when the weather changes. Many of us have a navigation system in our cars that monitors our speed, location, and progress toward our destination—and it notifies us when we've made a wrong turn or when there is heavy traffic en route. We monitor many conditions—some for safety reasons, others for comfort or convenience, and still others for targeted improvement.

We do not monitor these items just to collect and store data. As noted in another study of pedometers, monitoring leads to action (Weinstock et al., 2011). It seems reasonable, then, to suggest that schools use monitoring systems as part of their efforts to improve performance. And, similar to the reactions caused by studies of physical activity or a smoke detector going off, having the data in front of us should cause action. However, many sound improvement plans—instructional or otherwise—are rendered ineffective due to benign neglect. As with a New Year's resolution to increase your activity level, good intentions alone are not enough. Enrolling in a local gym with an excellent exercise program isn't enough if you rarely go. What's often missing is a way of monitoring progress en route. In this chapter, we will examine the processes and practices of developing a monitoring plan that equals the robustness of your instructional improvement plan.

Data Collection and Analysis

A good monitoring plan requires collecting data and dedicating time to analyze the results. The data collected need to be the right data, otherwise analysis will not yield relevant findings. The development of a monitoring plan should occur concurrently with goals, and the objectives and interventions need to be designed so the information collected aligns with desired outcomes. Used properly, data analyses should result in midcourse corrections that improve instruction and intervention. Formative assessments lie at the heart of a robust monitoring plan; note that formative assessments differ somewhat from the routine checking for understanding that effective teachers do as a part of their daily instruction (Fisher & Frey, 2007). Checking for understanding often includes using students' oral and written language production; asking questions to determine what they know and don't know; as well as using projects, performances, and tests to gauge their learning. These techniques are an important part of the continuous cycle of teaching, learning, and assessment that form the foundation of effective teaching. But a sound monitoring plan requires moving these decisions beyond the boundaries of a single classroom. The data collection and analysis needed must include multiple classrooms, organized primarily through professional learning communities. A chief method for organizing and collecting data is to use common formative assessments and consensus scoring to allow a team to draw conclusions about progress. Once the intervention plan discussed in Chapter 5 has been created, systems must be put in place to monitor it. Whether the team develops a schoolwide plan or a grade-level plan, a monitoring system must be in place to ensure the plan is implemented as intended and leads to the desired results.

Common Formative Assessments

One of the ways to monitor progress toward goals and objectives is to administer common formative assessments, which are given at the same time to all students enrolled in a specific grade or class. The use of common formative assessments requires that teachers focus on the same content at the same time, often through the creation of pacing guides. Using common formative assessments allow for the administration and scoring of assessments and then discussions about the results. The process we have outlined elsewhere includes the following steps (Fisher, Grant, Frey, & Johnson, 2007):

• **Step 1: Pacing Guides.** As an essential beginning point, groups of teachers who teach the same course (e.g., 4th grade, algebra, U.S. history, kindergarten, biology) meet and agree on pacing guides. Pacing guides identify when specific content standards are taught, which instructional materials can be used, and what types of instructional strategies can be deployed. In addition to these components, pacing guides can include key vocabulary terms that are required for understanding, formative and summative assessments used to determine student understanding, as well as accommodations that may be necessary for students with disabilities, universal access strategies for English language learners, or modifications for students performing above grade level.

• **Step 2: Common Formative Assessments.** In addition to the pacing guides that contain summative assessments, teachers in their course-alike groups design, develop, or modify assessment items that are subsequently administered to all students regardless of which teacher they have. The specific test items are developed so they will provide information to help the teachers determine what students are understanding, where there are gaps in comprehension or misunderstandings in learning, and who needs intervention and what type. As groups of teachers develop these assessment items, they learn more about the content standards and how those standards might be assessed. In addition, they plan distracter items designed to indicate when students overgeneralize, oversimplify, or exhibit common misunderstandings about the content. Students must understand tests as a genre, especially how they work and what to expect. However, common formative assessments should not be limited to items that emulate the state test. Short answer, timed essays, constructed response, and alternative response items can be included in common formative assessments.

- **Step 3: Item Analysis.** The third step occurs after a group of students has participated in the common formative assessment. In course-alike groups, teachers meet to discuss the results. Several software programs provide item-level analysis, which indicates the percentage of students who selected each of the distracters. Alternatively, groups of teachers can complete this analysis. The item analysis is critical as it allows teachers to look across the student body for trends—lessons that need to be retaught, assessment items that need changing, or pacing guides that need revision. The item analysis should also allow teachers to examine clusters of students, which is especially important in determining how a targeted group, such as English language learners, performed on a specific item. The item analysis is the key to instructional conversations and subsequent interventions.

- **Step 4: Instructional Conversations.** The instructional conversation is the reason why teachers do the work required by common formative assessments. Talking with colleagues who teach the same content and who see the same results is foundational to instituting instructional improvements. In course-alike groups, teachers can determine which instructional approaches are working, which instructional materials are effective, and which students still need help to master the standards. As we will see from the following examples, instructional conversations allow teachers to return to their individual classrooms and engage in the real work of formative assessments—to reteach and intervene when students don't do well.

For example, a group of 9th grade English teachers administered a common formative assessment focused on persuasive techniques. Overall, the students did very well, but a few questions seemed difficult for many of them. Most of the students selected the incorrect answer for this question:

Your friend wants you to listen to country music and says that you should because everyone else is doing it. This technique is called:

a) Plain folk

b) Emotional appeal

c) Testimonial

d) Bandwagon

During their discussion, the group of English teachers hypothesized about the thinking behind the number of students who selected "plain folk" rather than "bandwagon." One of the teachers noted, "I think that they probably thought that their friend was a regular person, and that was the first choice, so they picked it." Another added, "I bet if we didn't include plain folk but used a rhetorical question or card stacking instead, they would have gotten it right." A third teacher said, "But they really should have gotten this right. It's not plain folk. They missed the fact that it says that everyone else is doing it. But I am more concerned about their responses to question 32. Can we talk about that one when we have time?"

The conversation continued for several minutes, and the teachers decided they would add some additional practice to the spiral review homework about the ways in which people are persuaded to change their thoughts or habits. Then they could monitor students' continued understanding of the terminology. One teacher noted, "Our students did really well on this and just missed a couple of items. But I agree that adding this to their practice work at home will be useful in making sure that they don't forget it."

Their discussion turned to question 32, and the teachers noted that their students struggled with applying their knowledge.

32. The following is excerpted from Martin Luther King Jr.'s speech "I Have a Dream." Analyze the persuasive elements of this paragraph. What technique(s) is he using? Make sure that you defend your position. You may write about one or more techniques.

But one hundred years later, the Negro still is not free. One hundred years later, the life of the Negro is still sadly crippled by the manacles of segregation and the chains of discrimination. One hundred years later, the Negro lives on a lonely island of poverty in the midst of a vast ocean of material prosperity. One hundred years later, the Negro is still languishing in the corners of American society and finds himself an exile in his own land. So we have come here today to dramatize a shameful condition. (King Jr., 1963)

One of the teachers said, "I'm disappointed that they took the easy way out. Nearly every student talked about repetition and only repetition. I think that we need to review this and help them analyze speeches more carefully. They know so much more than this." As the 9th grade English teachers discussed the students' responses, they decided to plan some additional lessons about persuasive techniques. The teachers brainstormed additional speeches they could use for students to analyze. For example, one teacher suggested using a few of John F. Kennedy's speeches, including his "Inaugural Address" and the "Civil Rights Address"; another teacher suggested using Barbara Charline Jordan's

"Statement on the Articles of Impeachment." The teachers shifted their work to focus on what they wanted to teach next, based on their students' performance on the common formative assessment.

Benchmark Assessments

Usually designed by a district, state, or outside vendor, benchmark assessments are regularly spaced interim assessments that provide schools with information about students' progress toward standardized test outcomes. Most often, these benchmarks have been developed using the assessment blueprint of the summative test, and are intended to align to expected progress at specific points during the school year. The evidence on the use of benchmark assessments is mixed, with some studies showing little effect on instructional practices and student achievement, and others showing significant effects (Carlson, Borman, & Robinson, 2011). A factor that appears to make the difference lies in the ability of district- and building-level administrators and teachers to make data-driven decisions that result in changes to instruction. Most commonly, these instructional changes are evidenced in the identification of students who are lagging behind. The data analysis results may also alert teachers about curriculum gaps. In addition, there is speculation that exposure to benchmark assessments has a practice effect for students because it cognitively prepares them for the summative test (Carlson et al., 2011). Although it is not clear which of these factors or combinations of factors positively contribute to student achievement, it is certain that what educators do with the data plays an important part in the instructional improvements.

For instance, a district-developed benchmark assessment in mathematics includes color-coded reports on the progress of each student. The 3rd grade teachers use these twice-yearly administered benchmark results to plan for short-term interventions. The student names are color coded: green for students making expected progress, yellow for students slightly below expected levels, and red for students significantly below grade level. "When we first started getting these reports, we mostly looked at how our own classes were stacking up," said one teacher. Another continued, "But our school's data team showed us a different way of analyzing this." The 3rd grade teachers explained that they look at all the classrooms in the grade to figure out where to concentrate resources. "We're lucky enough to have a math specialist, but we used to think that we should all get the exact same amount of her time. Now we make a grade-level plan to figure out where the math specialist should spend her time," offered one teacher. In addition, the teachers have done some temporary regrouping of students for focused intervention time. "Twice a week we regroup so that the kids who are scoring below grade level on the benchmarks get additional developmental math support," said a 3rd grade teacher. "These lessons are taught by one of us and are aligned to the current standards we're working on, but with attention to the background knowledge they need." Another teacher said, "Like we're teaching about using place value strategically to add and subtract up to 1,000, but we've identified some students who are still working on identifying and skip-counting numbers up to 1,000. If they don't know this, they're lost on the new stuff we're teaching. So we're making sure they get some time for developmental math so we can accelerate their growth," she said. "We'll know more about whether this is effective when we analyze the next benchmark results in January."

Summative Assessments

Summative assessments, such as end-of-course exams and state accountability assessments, can also be used to monitor progress and to determine if objectives are met. Many times, school improvement plans focus on these more formal measures. Over many years, these assessments can be used to monitor progress, but they do not allow for monitoring much more frequently. So it is important to have objectives that allow for regular collection and review of data—typically monthly or more frequently.

When summative assessments are used to monitor progress over the long term, they should be discussed like common formative assessments and benchmark assessments. The key to this conversation is to focus on what can be learned from the data about improving the instructional program in the future. For example, when the teachers at Campbell Middle School reviewed their summative data, they focused on the trends. Their students' vocabulary and word analysis scores showed a consistent and steady decline at the same time that their writing conventions scores showed significant increase. The teachers wanted to know why the vocabulary and word analysis scores were declining and decided to focus on this topic, looking for root causes. As they investigated, they discovered that teachers across the content areas were teaching less vocabulary as new content assessments were being implemented. One of the science teachers noted, "I used to focus a lot more on vocabulary to help out the school scores overall. Now we have a cumulative science test and I really need to focus on the content." The team decided to take a second look at the summative data and more carefully analyze the science and social studies scores. To the team's surprise, the scores were flat. The same percentage of students scored proficient or advanced all three years that the assessments had been given. In reporting the findings to the larger faculty, the Title I teacher commented, "We're not getting any better or any worse in the areas of science and social studies. But we are getting worse in vocabulary overall. Maybe we need to make sure that students know a lot more words so that they have the background knowledge necessary to respond to any questions that they're asked. And, it's not like it will hurt them later in life, to know a lot more words." In response, several teachers voiced their support, including the science teacher who had once taught a lot more vocabulary, adding, "I think we need to step it up here and get back on that vocabulary train. I got off it, and it really didn't help. I hope you'll all join me."

In agreeing to focus on vocabulary again, the team members developed a new objective and created a progress monitoring plan. Their objective indicated "85 percent of students at Campbell will score 8 out of 10 on grade-level appropriate vocabulary assessments for five consecutive weeks." They decided to monitor the implementation of their plan by administering weekly vocabulary assessments as part of the English instruction and to conduct learning walks or walk throughs of the classrooms to check for implementation, which will be discussed later in this chapter.

Looking at Nonacademic Data

Thus far, we have focused on student achievement. However, if there are goals and objectives that focus on other factors of the school, these must be monitored as well. School climate, student attendance, discipline, and parent engagement are some of the other factors that are often included in instructional improvement intervention plans. As with student achievement, waiting until the end of the year to review data is too late. Each objective in the instructional improvement plan should be monitored regularly, which may mean analyzing attendance trends weekly, monitoring suspensions and expulsions monthly, or administering climate surveys quarterly.

For example, as part of their instructional improvement plan at Shiloh Elementary School, the team members focused on increased attendance. In their monitoring efforts, they reviewed attendance data weekly and used a database to determine which students had missed more than 10 percent of the school days. They printed that list each Monday to monitor the overall number of students who were missing school and to allow staff to intervene with the students immediately. Each week, three students on the list were visited at home. The content of the conversation focused on the importance of attending school and offered the family assistance in getting the student to school. On one visit, the team learned of a childcare need and was able to arrange for early start preschool services. On another visit, the team learned of a student's defiant behavior and helped the parents with a behavioral support plan. On yet another home visit, the team learned about a traumatic experience and offered condolences and gained understanding that the student would miss a few more days of school as the family dealt with the situation. The team also realized that the student would need ongoing support when she returned to school.

One of the objectives at the School for the Creative and Performing Arts focused on community engagement. The team wanted to ensure that a wide range of people from the community attended events, including parents, members of the artistic community, politicians, and local business members. For each event, a team collected detailed information about the attendees and compared attendance based on recruitment methods. A review of the events and data allowed targeted advertising, using the limited resources available, to effectively increase attendance at shows. In response to what the team learned from the data, the school used an e-mail list to recruit community members to attend the play, but used flyers posted in local businesses to recruit community members to attend an art show during which artwork could be purchased. One of the teacher leaders noted, "Our students really need an audience to make this experience real. We have a responsibility to create an authentic situation for our aspiring artists, and that includes more than fostering personal creativity. They need to have people in the theater, see people walking through the gallery, and interact with people who might not understand their artistic gifts."

A Calendar for Data Collection and Analysis

In the instructional improvement process, creating a calendar of events related to progress monitoring is important. Without a calendar that identifies when specific data will be collected and analyzed, the work is unlikely to occur because even the most dedicated and well-intentioned teams get busy and side-tracked. Without a calendar and a way of monitoring the intervention plan, the school may not reach the desired outcomes. Without a calendar of events, the team is unable to make midcourse corrections in the interventions.

The progress monitoring calendar should include all the assessments that are scheduled to be administered, as well as the timeline for collecting nonacademic indicators. In addition, the calendar should include timelines with specific dates on which teams will meet to review the results of these assessments or other indicators. Figure 6.1 contains a sample page from Grant Street Elementary School. The calendar includes weekly attendance reviews, the administration of at least one assessment per grade per month (including benchmark assessments and common formative assessments), deadlines

FIGURE 6.1
Sample Assessment Calendar

Sunday	Monday	Tuesday	Wednesday	Thursday	Friday	Saturday
		1 • Grade 2 Team meeting	2	3 • Grade 3 Common math assessment	4 • Quarterly climate survey sent	5
6	7 • Attendance review	8 • Grade 4 Common literacy assessment	9	10 • Grade 3 team meeting	11 • Data team meeting	12
13	14 • Kindergarten Benchmark attendance review	15 • Grade 4 Team meeting	16 • Grade 5 Common math assessment	17 • Grade 1 Benchmark	18 • Kindergarten Common math assessment	19
20	21 • Kindergarten team meeting • Attendance review	22	23 • Grade 5 Team meeting	24 • Grade 1 Team meeting	25 • Data team meeting • Kindergarten team meeting	26
27	28 • Attendance review	29 • Grade 2 Common literacy assessment	30			

for grade-level teams to review data, a date for climate survey, and formal data team meetings. The calendar is full of data collection and review information and may seem overwhelming. But at Grant Street, the teachers know when they agreed to administer specific assessments and when they will be provided time to meet and discuss the results of these assessments. The calendar helps to keep them on track, and they are able to use the information they collect to modify their intervention plans and to improve the instruction that their students receive.

Thus far, we have focused on using data to make decisions about the progress being made toward the goals and objectives that were developed as part of the overall improvement plan. These outcome and student learning measures can be supplemented by process measures, specifically walk throughs and talk throughs. Similar to the common formative assessments that teachers can use to determine if progress has been made, administrators, peer coaches, and team members can conduct walk throughs and talk throughs to monitor the surrogate measure of success—high-quality instruction.

Learning Walks

When it comes to instruction, classroom observations are key. However, conventional wisdom views instruction and observation as isolated from one another, with no clear link as to how one should affect the other. Observations are seen as descriptions of what occurred in one class on one day. But these observations can be marshaled through the use of instructional rounds that invite educators to look for patterns (City, Elmore, Fiarman, & Tietel, 2009). By gathering data for the purpose of revealing patterns of application, the unit of analysis is broader. Rather than spotlighting the practice of one teacher, the practices of teachers across a grade level or a department are illuminated. At the high school where three of us—Doug, Nancy, and Diane—work, we call these classroom observations *learning walks*. Before the walk, we select one item to observe that is typically tied to an improvement or intervention goal. We then visit several classrooms, but only discuss what we observe after every three or four classrooms. By adhering to this guideline, we reduce the temptation to talk about an individual teacher's practice and instead look for trends across classrooms. For example, we have conducted hard data learning walks to analyze the use of purpose statements, to measure the frequency and duration of student writing in classes, and to quantify methods of student interaction instructional routines.

The composition of the learning walk team has been vital to the process. Ours always include teachers. The sight of a group of administrators walking into a classroom is needlessly stressful and reinforces the administration versus teaching staff mindset. We maintain a minimum 1:1 ratio of administrators and teachers to ensure that the observations and discussions are rich. At times, teachers and coaches will conduct learning walks without administrators. We have found that these informal hard data learning walks have increased the amount of communication among the faculty at the school, and have made decisions about instructional improvements more equitable and timely. Our colleague Bonnie McGrath (our principal) likes to remind groups that the time spent in a classroom does not constitute the entire process, and that "the talk through is more important than the walk through."

Learning walks can be intimidating for a school staff that has never done them before. The exercise has a learning curve, and professional development about the process should occur in advance of the first learning walk. Cheryl worked with an elementary school just beginning to use this process. A core team of teachers on the school's instructional leadership team began by conducting a learning walk in one another's classrooms while the students were at recess. The idea was spurred by a recent professional development session that encouraged the use of a focus wall for reading comprehension. The group decided to do an environmental check on the implementation and use of the focus wall. Each host teacher showed her focus wall to the team and briefly discussed how she used it in instruction. Although small, this check of focus walls was a first step in using learning walks. The team members debriefed after every third classroom and then discussed their impressions of the overall process when they had finished. They were surprised to discover just how beneficial the process was to each of them personally, and vowed to share their experiences with the entire staff and expand the process to include more classrooms. This *ghost walk* of classrooms, void of students, was designed as an early part of the process of building capacity for the school's leadership team and has since become another tool for gathering data.

As building leadership teams become more comfortable with ghost walks, they should begin conducting *capacity-building learning walks* during live teaching. Again, the team must meet in advance to determine a problem of practice (City et al., 2009). Determining the focus of the learning walk is critical to the process so that members of the team do not inadvertently begin assessing all aspects of the learning environment and thus dilute the data. We all have our own lens for looking at classroom practice. One person may be particularly attenuated to the tone of verbal interactions between the teacher and students, while another may pay close attention to the complexity of texts used in the lesson. Still another member may be watching closely for opportunities for English-language learners to use academic language, while a fourth member is sensitive to the classroom climate as it applies to students with disabilities. These are all valid observational purposes, but diverse data become impossible to examine and use constructively. What do you do with data when everyone is looking in a different direction? In terms of research methodology, this problem relates to interrater reliability. To ensure that a level of homogeneity exists among members, the problem of practice must be clearly defined. By taking the time to identify the focus, the team guarantees that a sufficient volume of targeted data is gathered to discuss.

Learning walks should not be limited to data teams, but should eventually be a part of the professional life of every teacher on campus. After sufficient professional development about the theory and practices of learning walks, every teacher on campus should participate in the process at least once per year. These *faculty learning walks* are facilitated by an administrator and are scheduled during teachers' planning times or other agreed upon times. As with other types of learning walks, defining the problem of practice is vital. In addition, the facilitator leads the discussion after every third or fourth classroom and discourages evaluative statements when offered. Faculty learning walks build the capacity of every teacher on campus to collect data, notice trends, and respond to them. They also lower the affective filter of teachers whose classrooms are the subject of a learning walk, because they understand the purpose and the outcomes.

Learning walks can expand beyond the boundaries of a single campus. We invite administrators from other buildings to serve as outside observers, because those not deeply entrenched in the day-to-day life of a school can offer different perspectives for the leadership or data monitoring team to consider. These *external eyes learning walks* consist of administrators from neighboring schools, sometimes called networks, who walk a building together to provide feedback to the building administrator. Because the principal at a building may be tempted to provide information beyond what is observed, we advise that an outside member serve as the facilitator. Once again, identifying the problem of practice is the starting point. For example, in a cluster of schools in San Diego, the administrative teams decided to focus on the lesson purpose, the role of the students and teacher during instruction, and evidence of critical thinking, creativity, and problem-solving skills. They designed a data collection sheet that only allowed for comment on those practices (see Figure 6.2).

FIGURE 6.2
Observation Tool

Teacher: _____   Observer: _____

Date: _____   Time: _____

What is the purpose of the lesson?
What is the role of the student in the instructional process? (*What are students doing?*)
What is the role of the teacher in the instructional process? (*What is the teacher doing and saying?*)
Evidence of critical thinking, creativity, and problem-solving skills.

All administrators engage in learning walks to provide feedback to individual teachers. Traditionally these are done in isolation, but we encourage the principal and the assistant principal to conduct these walks together as *collaborative learning walks*. As with the other types of learning walks discussed here, we believe that the opportunities to communicate with another person vastly expands your understanding of what is being observed. The purpose and the follow-up differ, as the feedback is largely for observed teachers. However, collaborative learning walks can be strengthened by determining in advance what the problem of practice will be and can help administrators refrain from making global (and somewhat general) observations about a classroom. In addition, the follow-up conversations with observed teachers should be collaborative, with both administrators present.

A final kind of learning walk is the *guided visit*. At the Health Sciences High School, we are often contacted by other schools interested in examining our practices. Although we are honored to share our practices with others, we are cautious about strangers evaluating our teachers. Over time we have developed a process for hosting schools for guided visits. About two weeks before the visit, we meet with the visiting team members virtually or in person to facilitate a discussion and to aid them in identifying their problem of practice. At that time, we can instruct the visiting team members about the purposes of a guided visit, as well as its limitations. In addition, we encourage them to link their problem of practice to a future professional development outcome. Here are examples of statements that visiting teams have developed:

• Examine the ways content area teachers use productive group work, so we can develop a professional development session on the topic for our school.

• Observe how staff interactions contribute to school climate, so we can compare these findings to those at our school.

• Analyze how the school's mission statement is actualized in policy and practice, so we can examine alignment at our school.

We view these guided visits as valuable opportunities for our own continuing professional development. For this reason, we invite teachers on their prep periods to join the visiting team, and more often than not include a few of our students. Including more than one type of stakeholder encourages the visitors to seek out multiple perspectives about what they are seeing. In addition, we arrange a lunch period for the visitors hosted by the students, so their team can ask candid questions. Of course, this effort takes quite a bit of trust within our building, and at first we did not involve students. For us, the process has evolved as we have built our own capacity through faculty walks. We are currently exploring the use of *student learning walks* at our school, beginning with the cadre of 11th and 12th grade student workers, education interns, and peer teachers.

All these learning walks are of limited value if an outcome for the talk-through dimension to the process isn't present. It is important to consider how, and with whom, the findings of the learning walk will be shared. In many cases, the findings are shared with the entire faculty, which serves a dual purpose: it builds the capacity of the staff for future learning walks, and it fosters a mindset of continuous monitoring of goals. With whom the findings are shared might be shaped by the stated problem of practice. For instance, a few members of the 9th grade team conducted a learning walk of 10th grade classrooms immediately after the first semester to analyze the alignment of practices so that they could adjust student preparation for the next year. They shared their findings with the 10th grade teachers and the other members of the 9th grade team so the groups could engage in a collective discussion of current practices and expectations. The conversation was mutually beneficial, and the 10th grade team responded by conducting a similar learning walk of the 9th grade classrooms near the end of the school year to gain a better sense of what the incoming students would be prepared to do. A summary of the different types of learning walks, purposes, membership, and follow-up appears in Figure 6.3.

Instructional Improvement in Action

Over the course of a few weeks, the data team members, including Principal Mario Marcos, constructed a calendar for the formative benchmark assessments the school would be using to monitor progress on the four goals. The major instructional goal—to improve mathematics achievement for this year's 4th grade students—included scheduled time during the first week of school to administer a math assessment to determine which students would benefit from intervention. The data team also identified dates for monthly formative assessments and the district's two benchmark assessments. "Don't forget that we need to block out time for data analysis and reporting in the PLCs," one member said. In addition, all teachers were scheduled for professional development on academic language for English learners, and given assignments for interim learning walks to monitor how these strategies were being put into practice and to identify areas where additional coaching might be needed.

FIGURE 6.3

Types of Learning Walks

Kind of Walk	Purpose	Time	Participants	Follow-Up Activities
Ghost Walk	To examine classrooms without students present to collect evidence of the school's identified problem of practice (Accountability/PD)	1 hour	Any walkthrough team; may include principal, assistant principal, teachers, PLC, central services, parents, consultants, staff developers	Summary of data collected: Evidence and Wonderings processed with entire faculty
Capacity-Building Learning Walks— Building Leadership Team Goes First	To collect data looking for evidence of the implementation of effective practices (Accountability/PD)	1 hour	Principal, assistant principal, and other members of the building leadership team	Summary of data collected: Evidence and Wonderings processed with entire faculty
Faculty Instructional Rounds/ Learning Walks	To involve entire faculty in visiting classrooms looking for evidence and collecting data around the school's identified Problem of Practice (Accountability/PD)	All day	Principal, assistant principal, and whoever is available each period and/or time segment, ultimately involving entire faculty throughout the year	Summary of data collected: Evidence and Wonderings processed with entire faculty
External Eyes	To provide a fresh perspective looking for evidence of identified problem of practice ("Look-fors") (Accountability/PD)	2 to 3 hours	Building principal and/or assistant principal with outside team of principals and teachers—with school members as guides	Summary of data collected: Evidence and Wonderings processed with entire faculty
The walks listed below may or may not be a part of teacher evaluation.				
Collaborative Administrator Walk throughs	To provide positive and critical feedback regarding the target of the walk for the purpose of improvement of instruction and/or employment decisions (Accountability/PD)	2 to 3 hours	Principal and assistant principal	Individual feedback
The Guided visit walk is designed for the learning of the visiting team.				
Guided Visit	Visitors learn from the host school by viewing practices and collecting evidence to take back to their school (PD)	3 hours	Building principal and/ or assistant principal and small teams from different schools	Summary of data collected: Evidence and Wonderings for the visiting team to take away

Source: © 2013 by Bonnie McGrath. Used with permission.

The second goal, to reduce suspension and expulsion rates, would require a completely different monitoring system. "We're going to need monthly incidence reports submitted to the committee," said Mr. Marcos. "I'd like this committee to work like a medical review board. Let's schedule dates for this committee to meet with involved parties to examine the circumstances leading up to each event. I think as time goes we'll be able to uncover patterns and become more responsive." The team also noted that restorative practices training was a part of the plan. "Since this is an exploratory year, I'd suggest collecting surveys at the end of each session, and conducting some focus group interviews throughout the year to see how it's going," offered the counselor on the team. The others revisited the goal and identified several focus groups that would be excellent informants on the process, including students. "They can tell us best about positive or negative changes they're noticing," said another data team member.

The data team then turned its attention to the school's third goal, to improve family participation. "This looks like it needs monitoring quarterly," said a member. "We'll need to look at the rate of contacts we make as measured by newsletters, but also the ways that teachers are making those weekly contacts. We said that part of this intervention would be making at least two phone calls or sending at least two e-mail messages to each parent," said a teacher, "so we'll need to monitor that." Other members nodded their heads in agreement, but also wondered how they might do so. "We don't need teachers to complete one more report," Mr. Marcos observed, "but it does seem like an appropriate discussion for PLCs. What if we asked the PLCs to make this a standing agenda item at their meetings?" Others nodded in agreement. "And let's not forget the survey we asked the parent–teacher organization to conduct," said another teacher. "Let's figure out a deadline for when we need the PTO to administer and compile data, and schedule a time to hear findings. Based on what we learn, we may need to rethink our plan."

Having designed a monitoring plan for family participation, the data team looked again at the final goal, to improve attendance. "We're going to need a weekly data sweep for this one, or else the administrative team won't be able to respond in a timely manner," said a front office clerk. "I already run the attendance reports, so this should be something I do. Make it my responsibility to get the previous week's attendance data out to the administrators by 9:00 a.m. on Monday." "Don't forget us!" said the counselor and the social worker almost at once. "Let's hold a short meeting at 9:30 a.m. every Monday so we can figure out who needs to do what," Mr. Marcos said. With that, the data team reviewed its work on developing a calendar for collecting and analyzing data.

Team members noticed they had nearly forgotten one essential item—reporting these measures to the entire staff. They added reports on the four goals as standing items to every faculty and staff meeting. "None of these will take very long, especially if we're making sure these reports happen every two weeks," Mr. Marcos noted. "It will also keep us thinking about the kinds of questions or conclusions that others have when they look at data."

Quality Assurance

A plan is only as good as the monitoring that accompanies it. Even the most well-thought-out goals and robust interventions are likely to fall by the wayside without plans to revisit them. The fact is that once the school year is in full swing, many day-to-day events distract us from our long-range goals, and it is easy to put off monitoring for a better time that never arrives. In addition, we can approach the new school year with the best of intentions about collaboration, but lose sight of its purpose until we can only see a seemingly endless list of meetings that we are required to attend. Benchmark assessments are a good example of this phenomenon; if we forget their purpose, they begin to resemble "just another test" and we resent the time it takes away from instruction. In other words, we forget that assessment is a part of instruction. As you develop a monitoring plan, consider these quality assurance questions:

• Does every measure in your plan have a parallel plan for administering, analyzing, and reporting the findings?

• Are the findings shared with appropriate stakeholders (not just the data team)?

• Is there a monitoring calendar that thoughtfully spaces these assessments to maximize their usefulness?

• Does the monitoring plan allow for the school to revisit its goals to make mid-course adjustments?

• Do stakeholders have professional development needs to better collect, analyze, and report on the data? If so, has a timeline been developed to meet these needs?

7

Fast Forward: The Ongoing Pursuit of Excellence

Throughout this book, you have followed the journey of Mario Marcos's first year as the principal at an elementary school. When we first met Mr. Marcos in Chapter 2, he had just received his new assignment and was joining an existing leadership team. He guided the team and the school through a look at the hard and soft data available using visual displays, and together they decided to collect additional information. By Chapter 4, they had tentatively selected areas of concern and analyzed each for possible root causes. This analysis allowed them to design interventions that aligned with these root causes. In Chapter 5, he and the data team led a process involving the entire faculty and staff to develop interventions and create a plan for improvement. Soon after, a parallel monitoring component was added to the plan to ensure that these efforts did not fall by the wayside. But what happened to the instructional improvement plan? Was it effective? Were any efforts sustained? Let's fast forward two years to examine what occurred after the development of the plan.

Year 1: Implementing the Plan

The elementary school identified four areas of improvement: raising the 4th grade cohort's math achievement scores, decreasing suspension and expulsion rates, improving family participation and engagement, and improving attendance for a targeted group of habitually absent students. But several weeks into the school year, it was beginning to feel like writing the plan was the easy part; implementing it was proving more difficult.

Improving math achievement. The 4th grade teachers administered a county math test during the first week of school and were surprised by the results. Although they had known that this group of students had scored much lower than other cohorts for the last two years, they were nonetheless caught off-guard. "The sheer number of students who needed intervention was much larger than we had anticipated," said one 4th grade teacher. "Initially, we thought that we would be able to cluster the struggling students into one class twice a week for some developmental math work. We realized that wasn't going to work." The teachers quickly convened a meeting with the math specialist and Mr. Marcos to reevaluate their plan. Together they decided that for the first quarter, there would be a strong and purposeful thread of developmental math present in all lessons, for all students. Their intent was to get as many students up to speed as they could, so that they could concentrate more intensive intervention efforts later for students who continued to struggle. "We used the first two months of formative assessment tests, and then the first quarter district benchmark test to monitor individual students," said the math specialist. This approach worked, and as they entered the second quarter, a more manageable number of students emerged who would need long-term intervention. Reflecting on the year, a teacher said, "We returned to our original intervention plan, which was developmental math lessons delivered twice a week for these students, primarily in temporary whole group and small group lessons."

As the second quarter ended, a smaller number of students were identified for more formal response to instruction and Tier 2 RTI efforts. "We began to see that the student cohort was emerging across two categories: a large number who benefited from some initial reteaching of previous content during the first quarter, and a smaller group of students who needed some additional supplemental instruction during the second quarter," the math specialist offered. Another teacher continued, "By the end of the first semester, we could see which students were emerging as needing more intensive instruction." As the year progressed, two students were eventually referred for special education testing. The math specialist explained, "We felt really solid about those referrals because we had been systematically following their progress for so long. When they qualified for extra supports and services, we felt like we were ahead of the game, since we already had a handle on how to best deliver these in the general education classroom."

The 4th grade team also joined the other grade levels in an ongoing professional development effort focused on academic language development. Mr. Marcos picks up the discussion, "When we first developed this plan, we were thinking that it was for the school's English learners. Over time, we began to realize that this was beneficial for all the students in the school." In partnership with the district's English learner program coordinator, the 4th grade team developed a calendar of professional development sessions, interspersed with learning walks. "That was a learning process in itself," he recalled. "It seemed so simple at first glance, but it took longer to build the kind of trust that was needed to make the most of these walks." Over the course of the year, every teacher in the school participated in ghost walks to look at how the environment could support academic language development. In addition, the building leadership team began learning walks in one another's classrooms. "Reporting our findings about our own classrooms to the rest of the faculty was huge," one member said. "I think that was the turning point for us in opening our doors to one another."

Later in the year, students sat for the state achievement tests. The 4th grade teachers held their collective breath: How would the students do? They were cautiously optimistic, as the data from the monthly formative assessments and the district benchmark tests showed steady gains. Later that summer, when the achievement data were released, they realized they had come close to achieving their goal of raising the number of students attaining proficient or advanced levels from 27 percent to 45 percent. The report showed that 43 percent of their students scored proficient or advanced. This increase was a cause for celebration, and also a reminder that, as one teacher offered, "We weren't done with this group yet."

Decreasing suspension and expulsion rates. The school had identified a sudden rise in the rate of suspensions and expulsions as a disturbing turn of events. Although not out of line with the district's overall numbers, it was a five-year high for the school. Impressively, the school did not wait to see if this rate increase would emerge as a trend— it responded swiftly. Recognizing that an improvement plan would require a multiyear effort, the committee charged with monitoring this goal engaged with the local university's counseling and school psychology department to conduct a long-term study around the development of restorative practices. This effort involved teaching students about the process of restorative practices as well as faculty and staff development in implementing restorative practices. Restorative practices are an alternative to punitive discipline and focus on offenders facing their victims and working to restore the community (see www.iirp.edu). During the first quarter, the school formed a restorative practices team of interested faculty and staff to build their expertise in responding to conflicts. "This proved to be one of the most important things we did," said one of the ground supervisors on the team. "This was a first step in making sure that all the discipline problems weren't just handed over to the vice principal to handle. I think she was relieved to know she had a whole team she could rely on."

The team followed up by monitoring progress, and the stated goal of a 40 percent decline for each quarter was more than met. "During the first quarter we hit those numbers, but by the fourth quarter we had a 78 percent decrease from the previous year. And I am happy to say we didn't have a single expulsion the entire year," Mr. Marcus beamed. "We also held a follow-up meeting with each family a month after the suspension so we could gauge what was working, and what wasn't. The soft data proved to be instrumental in making refinements to our processes."

Increasing family participation. "We thought this would be easy, but it was more complex than we realized," said the president of the school's parent–teacher organization. The school purchased the auto-dialer and text messaging system for making contact with families, and this part of the plan proved to be straightforward. After collecting telephone numbers from families interested in participating, the PTO and teachers quickly began to realize the system's potential. Originally used for school announcements, by the second quarter the school began using it to send weekly messages about home literacy and mathematics, tips for developing home language proficiency for families of English learners, and positive and encouraging communications. The response was overwhelmingly positive from their survey of participating families.

But what proved to be harder to implement were the suggestions gathered from the PTO's survey of families about ways to improve family engagement. "We quickly realized that the suggestions were all over the map," said the front office clerk, a member of this committee. "Some families are here all the time, mostly because a parent's schedule works for doing so, but other families just can't be here because their schedules don't line up." This committee had met its initial goal of increasing parent contacts, but "it's just the tip of the iceberg. We have to look at this more closely," the clerk said.

Improving attendance. The attendance committee had identified 10 habitually absent students before the first day of school. "We were ready for them," said the social worker, a member of this team. "We set up meetings with each family and student during the first two weeks of school. I think a lot of families were surprised to be talking about attendance, but on the other hand these meetings went well, because we weren't waiting for the problem to happen. And families didn't feel defensive because there wasn't a problem yet."

As stated in the monitoring plan, the school developed a monthly attendance report. In addition to the 10 students, other children were sometimes on the watch list. In some cases, the school was able to help a family solve a transportation or scheduling problem; in a few cases, there were health concerns. "We had seven students over the course of the year that we helped get diagnosed for asthma," said the school nurse. "This has triggered a lot of other school supports as well." In one case, a student was newly diagnosed with Type 1 juvenile diabetes. "The family didn't even know that their child could qualify for special education supports and services as Other Health Impaired," said the nurse. "We coordinated our efforts with the special education director to get this in place quickly."

By year's end, the number of absences among six of the original 10 students was reduced. One student moved to a nearby school in the district, and the team members were able to notify the receiving school about the child's chronic absences and efforts that had been made to reduce them. "We had some success before she moved. I hope we were able to provide some seamless supports for a family that's been fairly transient for the last few years," said the social worker. "When we know there's a problem, it's our duty to make sure that there's some stability for a family that has to deal with frequent changes."

Year 2: Sustaining the Effort

Mr. Marcos began his second year as principal with some momentum, especially due to the overall success of the instructional improvement plan. The year started in similar fashion: examining data to look for trends, successes, and gaps; identifying areas of concern and conducting root analyses of each, then developing goals and objectives. But when the data team wanted to develop entirely new goals, Mr. Marcos cautioned, "Just because it's a new school year doesn't mean we have to write entirely new goals. Let's look more closely at the ones we had from last year to see what needs to be continued, refined, or eliminated."

The examination of the previous year's math goal was a revelation. One teacher commented, "It looks to me like there are two separate goals that need to be continued, out of the one we wrote last year." In due order, the team recommended continuing intervention efforts with this cohort, now entering 5th grade. "We can't just wash our hands of them after one year and hope for the best," a 4th grade teacher added. "I'd like to collaborate with the 5th grade team to identify what worked and what didn't work." In addition, many members recognized that the work on learning walks had only just begun. "We need another year of capacity-building on this," said a 2nd grade teacher. "We need to get to the point where we can do learning walks on a regular basis, but it's going to take more practice."

The data team now turned its attention to the goal to reduce suspension and expulsion. "Boy, we really nailed this one!" exclaimed one member. "I think we can cross it off the list." But a member of the restorative practices committee disagreed. "I agree we more than met our goal, but it's still a professional development issue. The more I learn about this, the more complex it is. I'd like to meet with the other members of the restorative practices group so we can make some recommendations to all of you. Can we schedule something for next Thursday?" he asked.

The third goal of increasing parent contact and engagement caused much discussion. "It's true that we met the goal of increasing contacts, but the results of the parent surveys tell us that we need to do more," said Mr. Marcos. "We have working parents who can't be here during the school day, but would like more information about participating in their child's education. And we have a large number of families who need resources in other languages." The data team determined that it needed to collect additional information through focus group interviews with working families, as well as with families that speak languages other than English.

Finally, the data team examined the outcomes of the goal on increasing student attendance. "We experienced a lot of success with this one," said the social worker. "But we need to keep it going," added another member. After discussing the goal, the group realized that increasing student attendance no longer needed to be a goal, but rather a part of the procedures of school. "Every year we're going to have chronically absent students," said Mr. Marcos. "That shouldn't surprise us. By putting some policies and procedures in place, we can be proactive about the way we approach this."

By the following week, the team had listed the following action items, continuing the efforts begun the previous year:

- The 5th grade math cohort has responded positively to efforts begun last year to increase proficiency. Given the students' history of difficulty with mathematics, we need to sustain this effort.

- We have begun work schoolwide on restorative practices, which has resulted in a significant decline in last year's suspension and expulsion rates. The restorative practices team states that our efforts are still at the beginning stages, and that our efforts should be expanded to more direct student and family involvement in this initiative, as well as more specialized training for specific members of the faculty and staff. A concern is that without continuation and expansion, this initiative will collapse and we will regress to previous levels of suspension and expulsion.

• Family involvement and engagement is still relatively low among specific groups, especially working families whose schedules conflict with school schedules and families of English language learners. We have increased the number and methods of contact with families, but have not made significant inroads with these groups. A concern is that without more focused intervention, we will create a system that privileges certain families along economic and language issues, while marginalizing others.

In addition, the team identified a newer action item that had been embedded within last year's 4th grade math goal:

• We have begun using learning walks to improve classroom practice, but have not made expected progress in moving to more sophisticated uses of them. A concern is that without continued professional development and practice on using learning walks, our efforts to examine data collectively and to collaborate across grade levels will stagnate, and we will regress to isolated practices.

The data team also added a new instructional problem to the charts, one identified through its hard data analysis on last year's achievement test scores.

• Last year's students in grades 2, 3, 4, and 5 scored below expected levels on their use of literary response and analysis, as measured through cluster skills report. A concern is that students who do not possess these critical skills will score lower on other measures of achievement, and that this issue will be further magnified in middle school.

As it had done the previous year, the data team presented the hard and soft data to the faculty and staff and further refined these problem statements. Every adult on campus committed to examining a problem statement to identify root causes and to share them with one another. Based on these root causes, the committees, each led by a data team member, drafted possible interventions and presented them to the administrators, faculty, and staff, as well as the PTO. Within a month, a formal instructional intervention plan and parallel monitoring plan had been written. "It really is true that continuous improvement is in the air we breathe every day," Mr. Marcos commented later. "Instruction, assessment, improvement—they're all intertwined. It's our job to make sure that our improvement plans are fully aligned with what we do every day. Otherwise, those plans sit on a shelf in a binder."

Common Pitfalls in Instructional Improvement

In this book, we have outlined an instructional improvement process that leads to success for students. We've made this process sound fairly easy, and it is when the common pitfalls are avoided. Even so, it's not simple or fast. Instructional improvement has to become a way of life. It has to become the way that the school operates, and the way that the adults within the school interact with one another. In this section, we present some of the most common pitfalls that may need to be addressed if instructional improvement is going to become a reality.

Neglecting to collect information. One common pitfall that prevents school teams from focusing on instruction improvement is the lack of data. Too often, the only data that are available, or that are routinely collected, involve annual state assessment data. In some schools, data are returned at the start of the year, but no one ever looks at the information. In other schools, data are so limited that there cannot be a discussion of target groups or clusters of need. Having access to good information—data—is a prerequisite for instructional improvement.

Putting plans on the shelf. Another common pitfall is that teams write plans that are submitted to the district or state, and then those plans sit on a shelf someplace, never to see the light of day again. This problem happens so frequently that veteran teachers develop some healthy skepticism about the process of improvement. When a team decides to focus on instructional improvement, it has to make a commitment that it will work hard to implement the plan and revisit the plan often so that it does not reinforce the past practices of neglect.

Setting new goals every year. As teams analyze their data, they should develop goals and objectives for instructional improvement. However, some teams completely revise their goals each year, unintentionally sending the message that the goals from the previous year are no longer important and that the new goals are the exclusive focus. Instead, teams should build on the goals from previous years, or maintain the same goals and develop new objectives for those goals. In this way, the various stakeholders see the relationship between their past efforts and their current priorities.

Settling for good enough. Some schools, particularly those that meet federal or state designations suggesting that they have met the accountability demands, lack sufficient internal need to improve. In these schools, the stakeholders rest on their laurels because other schools are much lower performing. In reality, we should all focus on instructional improvement and continually strive for excellence. It's not enough to simply meet whatever the current definitions are of "good enough." Each faculty member and each staff member should strive to be his best self, and that requires continuous high-quality improvement efforts.

Forgetting to anticipate changes. Schools exist in a turbulent policy environment, with several system layers focusing on the next right thing that will make a difference. Everyone—local school boards, state boards of education, state and federal legislators, membership organizations, governors and their council, the federal department of education, policy and advocacy groups, the entire judicial system, parent groups—has an opinion and some influence on what happens in schools. The instructional improvement process should anticipate changes to the landscape, not simply reflect on what was. As we stated in the beginning of this book, driving a car requires more than looking in the rearview mirror. Systems that fail to anticipate changes will not use data to consider changes necessary to implement the Common Core State Standards, for example, or to consider how major political, social, and historical events will shape the curriculum and how it is assessed, or even how global competition and the skill sets needed for a global market affect curriculum, instruction, and assessment. A well-functioning team looks ahead, not just behind, to develop goals, objectives, interventions, and monitoring plans.

Privatizing practice. In too many places, classrooms are private places that require an appointment to visit. In some schools, teachers do not meet in professional learning communities to review student performance on common formative assessments and then decide what steps to take to address the needs they identify. In some schools, teachers have never seen their colleagues teach. For instructional improvement to really work, schools must deprivatize practice to allow an open exchange of information and ideas. Teachers should have time to collaborate, and should use that time to focus on students and their performance.

Overlooking the engagement of stakeholders. As we have noted earlier in this chapter, many different groups care about what happens in schools. In some places, family and community members, teachers, classified staff, administrators, and students are all involved in meaningful ways in instructional improvement. In other schools, the leadership team writes the plan and then shares it with teachers, who are significantly less likely to implement the plan. In other schools, there is a data team that develops the plan but does not involve the broader school community; parents and community members question what is going on within the school and are unsure how to help. In most schools, students are left out of the discussions about instructional improvement. In schools that continuously improve, stakeholders are engaged and understand how their role contributes to the implementation—and eventual success—of the instructional improvement efforts.

Missing the need to define quality. As we have noted throughout this book, focusing on the quality of instruction is critical in the instructional improvement process. In terms of instruction, administrators, peer coaches, and teachers must agree on a definition of high-quality instruction so they can interact with one another about the work of educating students. Without an agreed upon definition of high-quality instruction, feedback from peers or administrators is dismissed. When the person providing the feedback has a shared definition of high-quality instruction with the person receiving that feedback, the conversation is productive and results in change.

Quality Assurance

This book has focused on a process that schools can use to improve their instructional program. The process requires that hard and soft data are collected and analyzed, that goals and objectives are developed, and that improvement plans are designed, implemented, and monitored. Working through the described process allows schools to debug their operations by identifying problems that prevent students from achieving. Problems are relatively easy to find, and the people who work inside schools can often easily list a set of problems that need to be addressed. Solutions to problems are also relatively easy to identify, and the people who work inside schools can often easily list a set of solutions that could be implemented. The challenge is really sustaining focus and creating a feedback loop so the solutions are actually implemented to determine if they work.

As you consider your next steps for developing and implementing an instructional improvement process at your school, we remind you once more about asking those quality assurance questions you have seen throughout this book.

- Do we sustain change across school years, or do we only consider one school year at a time?
- Have we looked back at other school improvement efforts from our past to identify what has worked, and what hasn't?
- Are we anticipating pitfalls?
- Do we keep ourselves in a reactive state, or do we look forward in an effort to anticipate future changes?
- Do we have the right people at the table?
- Do we recruit the people we need from other stakeholder groups?
- Do we take the time to celebrate our gains?

As we noted in the opening of this book, data are available everywhere we look. By collaborating and working through the process outlined in this book, your school community can make great strides in educating successful cohorts of students—all simply by using data to focus instructional improvement. We've made this process sound easy, and it is. Sustaining attention and maintaining communication is a challenge, but you now have the knowledge to overcome obstacles and lead your school and students to increased success.

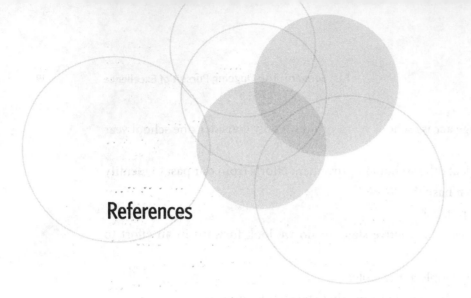

References

Allington, R. L., & Gabriel, R. E. (2012). Every child, every day. *Educational Leadership, 69*(6), 10–15.

Ammerman, M. (1998). *The root cause analysis handbook: A simplified approach to identifying, correcting and reporting workplace errors* (pp. 66–67). New York: Quality Resources.

ASQ. (2012). Quality assurance and quality control. Retrieved from http://asq.org/learn-about-quality/quality-assurance-quality-control/overview/overview.html

Bambrick-Santoyo, P. (2010). *Driven by data: A practical guide to improve instruction.* San Francisco, CA: Jossey-Bass.

Barrett, E. J., Ausbrooks, C. Y. B., & Martinez-Cosio, M. (2012). The tempering effect of schools on students experiencing a life-changing event: Teenagers and the Hurricane Katrina evacuation. *Urban Education, 47*(1), 7–31.

Basch, C. E. (2011). Asthma and the achievement gap among urban minority youth. *Journal of School Health, 81*(10), 606–613.

Black, P., & Wiliam, D. (1998). Assessment and classroom learning. *Assessment in Education: Principles, Policy and Practice, 5*(1), 7–74.

Bolman, L. G., & Deal, T. E. (2008). *Reframing organizations: Artistry, choice, and leadership.* San Francisco, CA: Jossey-Bass.

Borman, G., Slavin, R. E., Cheung, A., Chamberlain, A., Madden, N. A., & Chambers, B. (2007). Final reading outcomes of the national randomized field trial of success for all. *American Educational Research Journal, 44,* 701–731.

Boykin, A. W., & Noguera, P. A. (2011). *Creating the opportunity to learn: Moving from research to practice.* Alexandria, VA: ASCD.

Bravata, D. M., Smith-Spangler, C., Sundaram, V., Gienger, A. L., Lin, N., Lewis, R.,... Sirard, J. R. (2007). Using pedometers to increase physical activity and improve health. *Journal of the American Medical Association, 298,* 2296–2304.

Brophy, J. E. (1982). How teachers influence what is taught and learned in classrooms. *Elementary School Journal, 83*(1), 1–13.

California Department of Education. (2008). *Response to instruction and intervention*. Retrieved from http://www.cde.ca.gov/nr/el/le/yr08ltr1114att.asp

Carlson, D., Borman, G. D., & Robinson, M. (2011). A multistate district-level cluster randomized trial on the impact of data-driven reform on reading and mathematics achievement. *Educational Evaluation and Policy Analysis, 33*(3), 378–398.

Carpenter, T. P., Fennema, E., & Franke, M. (1996). Cognitively guided instruction: A knowledge base for reform in primary mathematics instruction. *Elementary School Journal, 97*, 3–20.

Carroll, L. (1993) *Alice's adventures in wonderland*. Mineola, NY: Dover.

Chetty, R., Friedman, J. N., & Rockoff, J. E. (2011). *The long-term impacts of teachers: Teacher value-added and student outcomes in adulthood*. Executive summary of National Bureau of Economic Research working paper no. 17699. Retrieved from http://obs.rc.fas.harvard.edu/chetty/value_added.html

Chun, H., & Dickson, G. (2011). A psychoecological model of academic performance among Hispanic adolescents. *Journal of Youth and Adolescence, 40*(12), 1581–1594.

City, E. A. (2011). Learning from instructional rounds. *Educational Leadership, 69*(2), 36–41.

City, E. A., Elmore, R. F., Fiarman, S. E., & Tietel, L. (2009). *Instructional rounds in education: A network approach to improving teaching and learning*. Cambridge, MA: Harvard Educational Press.

Creswell, M. (2008). *Research design: Qualitative, quantitative, and mixed methods approaches* (3rd ed.). Thousand Oaks, CA: Sage.

Croteau, R. J. (2010). *Root cause analysis in health care: Tools and techniques* (4th ed.). Oakbrook Terrace, IL: Joint Commission on Accreditation of Healthcare Organizations.

Crowson, R. (2003). *School-community relations under reform* (3rd ed.). Richmond, CA: McCutchan.

Darling-Hammond, L. (2000). Teacher quality and student achievement: A review of state policy evidence. *Education Policy Analysis Archives, 8(1)*, 1–49.

Darling-Hammond, L., Ancess, J., & Ort, S. W. (2002). Reinventing high school: Outcomes of the coalition campus schools project. *American Education Researcher, 39*(3), 639–673.

Darling-Hammond, L., & McLaughlin, M. W. (1995). Policies that support professional development in an era of reform. *Phi Delta Kappan, 76*(8), 597–604.

Deal, T., & Kennedy, A. (1982). *Corporate cultures: The rites and rituals of corporate life*. Reading, MA: Addison-Wesley.

DeLacy, M. (2004). The 'No Child' law's biggest victims?: An answer that may surprise. *Education Week, 23*(41), 40.

Dimmock, C., & Walker, A. (2005). *Educational leadership: Culture and diversity*. Thousand Oaks, CA: Sage.

Donohue, G. (2011, Aug. 17). *Goal setting–powerful written goals in 7 easy steps!* Retrieved from www.topachievement.com/goalsetting.html

DuFour, R., DuFour, R., Eaker, R., & Karhanek, G. (2004). *Whatever it takes: How professional learning communities respond when kids don't learn*. Bloomington, IN: Solution Tree.

Fiore, D. J. (2011). *School-community relations* (3rd ed). Berkeley, CA: Eye on Education.

Fisher, D., & Frey, N. (2007). *Checking for understanding: Formative assessment techniques for your classroom.* Alexandria, VA: ASCD.

Fisher, D., & Frey, N. (2008a). *Better learning through structured teaching: A framework for the gradual release of responsibility.* Alexandria, VA: ASCD.

Fisher, D., & Frey, N. (2008b). Homework and the gradual release of responsibility: Making "responsibility" possible. *English Journal, 98*(2), 40–45.

Fisher, D., & Frey, N. (2010a). *Enhancing RTI: How to ensure success with effective classroom instruction and intervention.* Alexandria, VA: ASCD.

Fisher, D., & Frey, N. (2010b). *Guided instruction: How to develop confident and successful learners.* Alexandria, VA: ASCD.

Fisher, D., & Frey, N. (2011). *The purposeful classroom: How to structure lessons with learning goals in mind.* Alexandria, VA: ASCD.

Fisher, D., Frey, N., & Lapp, D. (2009). Meeting AYP in a high need school: A formative experiment. *Journal of Adolescent and Adult Literacy, 52,* 386–396.

Fisher, D., Frey, N., & Pumpian, I. (2012). *How to create a culture of achievement in your school and classroom.* Alexandria, VA: ASCD.

Fisher, D., Frey, N., & Rothenberg, C. (2011). *Implementing RTI with English learners.* Bloomington, IN: Solution Tree.

Fisher, D., Grant, M., Frey, N., & Johnson, C. (2007). Taking formative assessments schoolwide. *Educational Leadership, 65*(4), 64–68.

Fisher, D., & Ivey, G. (2006). Evaluating the interventions for struggling adolescent readers. *Journal of Adolescent and Adult Literacy, 50,* 180–189.

Frey, N. (2010). Home is not where you live, but where they understand you. In K. Dunsmore & D. Fisher (Eds.), *Bringing literacy home* (pp. 42–52). Newark, DE: International Reading Association.

Frey, N., Fisher, D., & Everlove, S. (2009). *Productive group work: How to engage students, build teamwork, and promote understanding.* Alexandria, VA: ASCD.

Gawande, A. (2004, December 6). The bell curve. Retrieved from http://www.newyorker.com/archive/2004/12/06/041206fa_fact

Greenfield, T. A., & Klemm, E. B. (2001). When "good" school restructuring efforts still fail. *American Secondary Education, 30*(1), 2–25.

Gregory, A., Skiba, R. J., & Noguera, P. A. (2010). The achievement gap and the discipline gap: Two sides of the same coin? *Educational Researcher, 39*(1), 59–68.

Harrison, B. S. (1992). *Managing change in organizations.* Los Angeles, CA: Baskin-Robbins International.

Hempel, S. (2007). *The strange case of the Broad Street pump: John Snow and the mystery of cholera.* Berkeley, CA: University of California Press.

Hindman, A. H., & Morrison, F. J. (2011). Family involvement and educator outreach in Head Start: Nature, extent, and contributions to early literacy skills. *Elementary School Journal, 111*(3), 359–386.

Johnson, S. (2006). *The ghost map: The story of London's most terrifying epidemic—and how it changed science, cities, and the modern world.* New York: Penguin Books.

Jones, P., Carr, J., & Ataya, R. (Eds.). (2007). *A pig don't get fatter the more you weigh it: Classroom assessments that work.* New York: Teachers College Press

Joyce, B., & Showers, B. (2002). *Student achievement through staff development* (3rd ed.). Alexandria, VA: ASCD.

King, M. L., Jr. (1963). "I have a dream." Retrieved from http://abcnews.go.com/Politics/martin-luther-kings-speech-dream-full-text/story?id=14358231.

Leithwood, K., Louis, K., Anderson, S., & Walstrom, K. (2004). *How leadership influences student learning.* Ontario, Canada: Center for Applied Research and Educational Improvement & Ontario Institute for Studies in Education.

Lindsey, R. B., Robins, K. J. N., & Terrell, R. D. (2009). *Cultural proficiency: A manual for school leaders* (3rd ed.). Thousand Oaks, CA: Corwin.

Los Angeles County Office of Education. (2000). *Teacher expectations and student performance.* Los Angeles, CA: Author.

Marzano, R., Waters, T., & McNulty, B. A. (2005). *School leadership that works: From research to results.* Alexandria, VA: ASCD.

McCormack, S., & Ross, D. L. (2010). Teaching with technology. *Science Teacher, 77*(7), 40–45.

McNamee, A., & Mercurio, M. (2008). School-wide intervention in the childhood bullying triangle. *Childhood Education, 84*(6), 370–378.

Merriam, S. (2002). *Qualitative research in practice: Examples for discussion and analysis.* San Francisco, CA: Jossey-Bass.

Miles, S. B., & Stipek, D. (2006). Contemporaneous and longitudinal associations between social behavior and literacy achievement in a sample of low-income elementary school children. *Child Development, 77,* 103–117.

Minner, D. D., Levy, A., & Century, J. (2010). Inquiry-based science instruction—What is it and does it matter? Results from a research synthesis years 1984 to 2002. *Journal of Research in Science Teaching, 47,* 474–496.

Muijs, D., Harris, A., Chapman, C., Stoll, L., & Russ, J. (2004). Improving schools in socioeconomically disadvantaged areas—A review of research evidence. *School Effectiveness and School Improvement, 15*(2), 149–175.

Pearson, P. D., & Gallagher, M. (1983). The instruction of reading comprehension. *Contemporary Educational Psychology, 8,* 317–344.

Preuss, P. G. (2003). *School leader's guide to root cause analysis: Using data to dissolve problems.* Larchmont, NY: Eye on Education.

Reeves, D. (2005). Putting it all together: Standards, assessment, and accountability in successful professional learning communities. In R. Barth & B. Eason-Watkins (Eds.), *On common ground: The power of professional learning communities* (pp. 45–64). Bloomington, IN: Solution Tree.

Reeves, D. B. (2004). *Accountability in action: A blueprint for learning organizations* (2nd ed.). Englewood, CO: The Leadership and Learning Center.

Reisman, A. (2012). Reading like a historian: A document-based history curriculum intervention in urban high schools. *Cognition & Instruction, 30*(1), 86–112.

Rose, D. H., Meyer, A., Strangman, N., & Rappolt, G. (2002). *Teaching every child in the digital age: Universal design for learning.* Alexandria, VA: ASCD.

Sanders, W. (2000) Value-added assessment from student achievement data: Opportunities and hurdles. *Journal of Personnel Evaluation in Education, 14,* 329–339.

Schein, E. (1992). *Organizational culture and leadership* (2nd ed.). San Francisco: Jossey-Bass.

Shanahan, T., & Barr, R. (1995). A synthesis of research on reading recovery. *Reading Research Quarterly, 30,* 958–996.

Shulman, L. (1987). Knowledge and teaching: Foundations of the new reform. *Harvard Educational Review, 57*(1), 1–22.

Shumow, L., Lyutykh, E., & Schmidt, J. (2011). Predictors and outcomes of parental involvement with high school students in science. *School Community Journal, 21*(2), 81–98.

Stiggins, R. J. (2001). The principal's leadership role in assessment. *NASSP Bulletin, 85*(13), 13–26.

Thaler, R. H., & Sunstein, C. R. (2008). *Nudge: Improving decisions about health, wealth, and happiness.* New Haven, CT: Yale University Press.

Tschannen-Moran, M., & Tschannen-Moran, B. (2011). Taking a strengths-based focus improves school climate. *Journal of School Leadership, 21*(3), 422–448.

Tyre, A., Feuerborn, L., & Pierce, J. (2011). Schoolwide intervention to reduce chronic tardiness at the middle and high school levels. *Preventing School Failure, 55*(3), 132–139.

Van Driel, J. H., & Berry, A. (2012). Teacher professional development focusing on pedagogical content knowledge. *Educational Researcher, 41*(1), 26–28.

Varlas, L. (2012). Improving student writing through formative assessments. *ASCD Education Update, 54*(2). Retrieved from http://www.ascd.org/publications/newsletters/education-update/feb12/vol54/num02/Improving-Student-Writing-Through-Formative-Assessments.aspx

Vaughn, S., Hughes, M. T., Moody, S. W., & Elbaum, B. (2001). Instructional grouping for reading for students with LD: Implications for practice. *Intervention in School and Clinic, 36,* 131–137.

Volpe, R. J., Young, G. I., Piana, M. G ., & Zaslofsky, A. F. (2012). Integrating classwide early literacy intervention and behavior supports: A pilot investigation. *Journal of Positive Behavior Interventions, 14*(1), 56–64.

Warren, M. R. (2011). Building a political constituency for urban school reform. *Urban Education, 46(3),* 484–512.

Weinstock, R. S., Brooks, G., Palmas, W., Morin, P. C., Teresi, J. A., Eimicke, J. P.,... Shea, S. (2011). Lessened decline in physical activity and impairment of older adults with diabetes with telemedicine and pedometer use: Results from the IDEATel study. *Age and Aging, 40*(1), 98–105.

White, S. H. (2011). *Show me the proof! Tools and strategies to make data work for the Common Core State Standards.* Englewood, CO: Advanced Learning Press.

Wright, S. P., Horn, S. P., & Sanders, W. (1997). Teacher and classroom context effects on student achievement: Implications for teacher evaluation, *Journal of Personnel Evaluation in Education, 11,* 57–67.

Zau, A. C., & Betts, J. R. (2008). *Predicting success, preventing failure: An investigation of the California High School Exit Exam.* Sacramento, CA: Public Policy Institute of California.

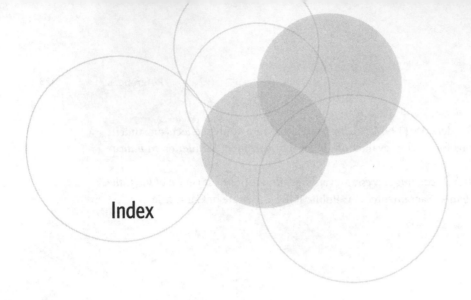

Index

Note: The letter *f* following a page number denotes a figure.

Cheryl James-Ward earned a bachelor's degree in Applied Mathematics from the University of California at Santa Barbara, a master's degree in Curriculum and Instruction from California State University Dominguez Hills, and a doctorate in education from the University of Southern California. She has served as both a principal and supervisor of schools for the Long Beach Unified School District. James-Ward is currently an assistant professor at San Diego State University and a leadership coach. Since 2003, she has coached more than 20 principals and assistant superintendents in districts throughout California. James-Ward may be contacted at cward@mail.sdsu.edu.

Douglas Fisher is a professor of educational leadership at San Diego State University and a teacher leader at Health Sciences High & Middle College. He is a member of the California Reading Hall of Fame and is the recipient of a Celebrate Literacy Award from the International Reading Association, the Farmer Award for Excellence in Writing from the National Council of Teachers of English, and a Christa McAuliffe Award for Excellence in Teacher Education from the American Association of State Colleges and Universities. Fisher has published numerous articles on improving student achievement, and his books include *The Purposeful Classroom: How to Structure Lessons with Learning Goals in Mind; Enhancing RTI: How to Ensure Success with Effective Classroom Instruction and Intervention; Checking for Understanding: Formative Assessment Techniques for Your Classroom;* and *How to Create a Culture of Achievement in Your School and Classroom.* He can be reached at dfisher@mail.sdsu.edu.

Nancy Frey is a professor in the School of Teacher Education at San Diego State University and a teacher leader at Health Sciences High & Middle College. Before joining the university faculty, Frey was a special education teacher in the Broward County (Florida) Public Schools, where she taught students at the elementary and middle school levels. Frey later worked for the Florida Department of Education on a statewide project for supporting students with disabilities in a general education curriculum. She is a recipient of the Christa McAuliffe Award for Excellence in Teacher Education from the American Association of State Colleges and Universities and the Early Career Award from the National Reading Conference. Frey's research interests include reading and literacy, assessment, intervention, and curriculum design. She has published many articles and books on literacy and instruction, including *Productive Group Work: How to Engage Students, Build Teamwork, and Promote Understanding; Guided Instruction: How to Develop Confident and Successful Learners;* and *Better Learning Through Structured Teaching: A Framework for the Gradual Release of Responsibility.* Frey can be reached at nfrey@mail.sdsu.edu.

Diane Lapp is a distinguished professor of education in the Department of Teacher Education at San Diego State University (SDSU), and has taught in elementary and middle schools. She is also an English/literacy teacher and instructional coach at Health Sciences High & Middle College. Lapp's major areas of research and instruction regard issues related to struggling readers and writers, their families, and their teachers. Coeditor of *Voices From The Middle,* published by National Council of Teachers of English, Lapp has authored, coauthored, and edited numerous articles, columns, texts, handbooks, and children's materials on reading, language arts, and instructional issues. She has also chaired and cochaired several committees for International Reading Association (IRA) and Literacy Research Association. Lapp's many educational awards include being named as the Outstanding Teacher Educator and Faculty Member in the Department of Teacher Education at SDSU, the Distinguished Research Lecturer from SDSU's Graduate Division of Research, IRA's 1996 Outstanding Teacher Educator of the Year, and IRA's 2011 Manning Award recipient for her work in public schools. She is also a member of both the California and the International Reading Halls of Fame. Lapp can be reached at lapp@mail.sdsu.edu.

Related ASCD Resources: School Improvement

At the time of publication, the following ASCD resources were available (ASCD stock numbers appear in parentheses). For up-to-date information about ASCD resources, go to www.ascd.org. You can search the complete archives of *Educational Leadership* at http://www.ascd.org/el.

Align the Design: A Blueprint for School Improvement by Nancy J. Mooney and Ann T. Mausbach (#108005)

Advancing Formative Assessment in Every Classroom: A Guide for Instructional Leaders by Connie M. Moss and Susan M. Brookhart (#109031)

Checking for Understanding: Formative Assessment Techniques for Your Classroom by Douglas Fisher and Nancy Frey (#107023)

Collaborative Analysis of Student Work: Improving Teaching and Learning by Georgea M. Langer, Amy Bernstein Colton, and Loretta S. Goff (#102006)

Enhancing RTI: How to Ensure Success with Effective Classroom Instruction and Intervention by Douglas Fisher and Nancy Frey (#110037)

The Learning Leader: How to Focus School Improvement for Better Results by Douglas B. Reeves (#105151)

Managing Diverse Classrooms: How to Build on Students' Cultural Strengths by Carrie Rothstein-Fisch and Elise Trumbull (#107014)

Mobilizing the Community to Help Students Succeed by Hugh B. Price (#107055)

Protocols for Professional Learning by Lois Brown Easton (#109037)

Reaching Out to Latino Families of English Language Learners by David Campos, Rocio Delgado, and Mary Esther Soto Huerta (#110005)

Strengthening and Enriching Your Professional Learning Community: The Art of Learning Together by Geoffrey Caine and Renate N. Caine (#110085)

Teaching Every Student in the Digital Age: Universal Design for Learning by David H. Rose, Anne Meyer, Nicole Strangman, and Gabrielle Rappolt (#101042)

Transformational Teaching in the Information Age: Making Why and How We Teach Relevant to Students by Thomas R. Rosebrough and Ralph G. Leverett (#110078)

Transformative Assessment by W. James Popham (#108018)

Transformative Assessment in Action: An Inside Look at Applying the Process by W. James Popham (#111008)

Transforming Professional Development into Student Results by Douglas B. Reeves (#109050)

Transforming Schools: Creating a Culture of Continuous Improvement by Allison Zmuda, Robert Kuklism, and Everett Kline (#103112)

Turning High-Poverty Schools into High-Performing Schools by William H. Parrett and Kathleen M. Budge (#109003)

Using Data to Assess Your Reading Program by Emily Calhoun (#102268)

What Every School Leader Needs to Know About RTI by Margaret Searle (#109097)

What Teachers Really Need to Know About Formative Assessment by Laura Greenstein (#110017)

THE WHOLE CHILD The Whole Child Initiative helps schools and communities create learning environments that allow students to be healthy, safe, engaged, supported, and challenged. To learn more about other books and resources that relate to the whole child, visit www.wholechildeducation.org.

For more information: send e-mail to member@ascd.org; call 1-800-933-2723 or 703-578-9600, press 2; send a fax to 703-575-5400; or write to Information Services, ASCD, 1703 N. Beauregard St., Alexandria, VA 22311-1714 USA.